STUDY GUIDE

TO ACCOMPANY

PUBLIC FINANCE:
A CONTEMPORARY APPLICATION OF THEORY TO POLICY

sixth edition

DAVID N. HYMAN
NORTH CAROLINA STATE UNIVERSITY

The Dryden Press

Fort Worth   Philadelphia   San Diego   New York   Orlando   Austin   San Antonio
Toronto   Montreal   London   Sydney   Tokyo

Address for Editorial Correspondence
The Dryden Press, 301 Commerce Street, Suite 3700, Fort Worth, TX 76102

Address for Orders
The Dryden Press, 6277 Sea Harbor Drive, Orlando, FL 32887
1-800-782-4479, or 1-800-433-0001 (in Florida)

ISBN: 0-03-021309-6

Printed in the United States of America

9 0 1 2 3 4   202   9 8 7 6 5 4 3 2

The Dryden Press
Harcourt Brace College Publishers

Preface

This study guide is designed to supplement the material presented in David N. Hyman's *Public Finance* (sixth edition). Each chapter begins with a list of chapter objectives, highlighting major concepts which the student should understand after reading and working through the textbook and study guide chapters. A chapter summary is then presented. This summary in no way substitutes for a careful reading of the chapter, but provides an additional means of summarizing some of the highlights of the textbook chapter. An Issue in Brief in each chapter focuses on a timely application of the material. Each Issue in Brief is also followed by several discussion questions to stimulate further thinking about the issue. The heart of each study guide chapter is the chapter review questions. True/false questions, multiple-choice questions, short-answer questions, and problems all provide opportunities for the student to test his or her knowledge of the chapter's material. The short-answer questions are also an excellent preparation for course discussion. answers to the chapter review questions are provided at the end of each chapter in the study guide. The final portion of each chapter is fairly unique. This Chapter Recap has the student write out answers to questions directly tied to the chapter objectives. This capstone not only helps the students to find out how well they have captured the key concepts of the chapter but also provides an excellent review tool for students to use as they prepare for course examinations.

David N. Hyman
Michael T. Peddle

Contents

CHAPTER 1

Individuals and Government

Chapter Objectives: After reading this chapter, you should understand:

1. The general parameters of public finance as a field of economic study.

2. The relative size of government in the United States, both historically and currently.

3. The relationship between government, political institutions, and collective choice as they relate to economics.

4. How the provision of government goods and services through political institutions differs from market provision of goods and services.

5. The measurement of the opportunity cost of governmental activity.

6. The circular flow in a mixed economy.

7. The difference between government purchases and transfer payments.

8. The structure of government expenditures and revenues in the United States.

9. Basic reasons for governmental activity.

Chapter Summary

1. Public finance is the field of economics that studies government activities and their economic basis, as well as the alternative means of financing government expenditures. It focuses on an under-standing of the economic role of government and its impact on the well-being of citizens. Public finance focuses on the role that governments play in allocating resources and the interrelationship between government activities and the choices of individual economic actors.

2. Public finance asks how much governments should do and how much should be left to private enterprise. Answering this question requires considering government's role as it is developed through political institutions, as well as collective choice, non-market rationing approaches to allocating resources. The extent to which individuals have the right to participate in decisions that determine what governments do varies from society to society.

3. In public finance, we view the opportunity costs of allocating resources between government and private use from the perspective of the value of the private goods and services forgone when resources are allocated to the public sector. Hence, government represents an additional resource-using body in our conventional circular flow model, participating in markets as the buyer (and sometimes seller) of goods and services. Using a conventional production possibilities frontier, the tradeoff between government goods and services and private goods and services can be established and illustrated.

4. *Private goods and services* are usually made available for sale in markets. *Public goods and services* are generally distributed to groups of individuals through non-market rationing.

5. A *pure market economy* is one in which goods and services are almost exclusively supplied by private, unfettered firms who sell their output in markets where prices are determined by the free operation and interaction of supply and demand. A *mixed economy* is one in which government supplies a considerable amount of goods and services and regulates private economic activity.

6. Government spending may either involve diversion of resources from private use to public use (government purchases for consumption and investment) or redistribution of the command over resources, that is, purchasing power, from one private user to another (*transfer payments*). In the United States there has been a significant shift in federal government expenditures toward transfers, though this trend somewhat reversed itself during the mid-1980s and returned to its upward path in the 1990s.

7. Since government output is not sold in markets or easily quantifiable in objective units, it is virtually impossible to measure government output. However, we often use total expenditures as an imperfect proxy. During the 1990s, government expenditures comprised about one-third of GDP. Since 1930, the role of the federal government in the economy has expanded at a much more rapid rate than that of state and local governments. The proportion of GDP accounted for by government expenditures in the United States is still low compared to other industrial nations whose government sectors also continue to grow.

8. Objects of spending tend to vary by level of government. The federal government now spends the largest portion of its revenue on social security (22%). National defense comprised 17% of federal expenditures in 1996, income security programs nearly 15%. Net interest paid is 14% of expenditures. (lower interest rates in the 1990s contributed to relative declines in net interest paid as a percentage of federal expenditures). At the federal level, transfer payments have risen to 45% of total government expenditures. On the other hand, education is the dominant expenditure category for state and local governments. Other major categories of state and local expenditure include health and hospitals, public safety, transportation, and income support/welfare.

9. The relative importance of revenue tools also varies by level of government. The federal government relies on payroll taxes, personal income taxes, and the corporate income tax for over 90% of its receipts. The federal government has also relied on borrowing as a source of revenue from 1970 to 1997 when it had large budget deficits. For state and local governments combined, the sales tax, property taxes, and the personal income tax are prominent sources of revenue, with grants from the federal government also extremely important.

10. Important functions of government include establishing property rights and enforcing contracts, redistributing income and economic opportunity among citizens, stabilization of economic fluctuations, regulation to maintain competition and health/safety, and provision of goods and services which are underproduced by the market.

Issue in Brief: Aging of the Population

The *Public Policy Perspective* on page 24 of the text indicates some of the fiscal problems that will result from the aging of the population in the United States. Aging of the population will mean that the proportion of retirees receiving tax-financed pensions and medical benefits will rise. At the same time the ratio of workers to retirees will decline. This implies that there will be relatively fewer taxpayers paying taxes to finance retirement benefits and other public services for a larger number of retirees. Aging of the population is probably going to be the most important influence on government spending in the next century.

Questions for Discussion:

1. What portion of federal spending now goes to programs that benefit people over the age of 65?

2. How will aging of the population increase government spending?

3. What will happen if spending on programs that benefit people over the age of 65 are not curtailed in the future?

CHAPTER REVIEW QUESTIONS

True/False Questions: If false, explain how to correct the statement to make it true.

_T_ 1. The majority of government expenditures are financed by taxes.

_T_ 2. Collective choices refer to decisions made through political institutions.

_F_ 3. Typically, government goods and services are distributed through markets.

_F_ 4. The United States and most other Western nations today are pure market economies.   Mixed

_F_ 5. Government purchases of defense equipment is an example of a transfer program.

_F_ 6. As a proportion of GDP, state and local government expenditures are greater than federal government expenditures in the United States.

_F_ 7. In the United States government expenditures account for a higher proportion of GDP than governments in most other industrialized nations.

_T_ 8. As a proportion of GDP, the federal government has only begun its growth in this century.

_T_ 9. Transfer payments now constitute a larger percentage of government expenditures in the United States than do government purchases for consumption and investment.

_T_ 10. Recent trends have shown an increase in federal grants to state and local governments as a share of GDP.   OLD trend

_F_ 11. National defense is the largest general expenditure category for our federal government.   Transfer Pmts

_T_ 12. Interest on the national debt in 1996 was the third largest category of annual expenditure for the federal government.

_F_ 13. Taxes paid and the benefits of government goods and services received tend to be directly related.

_T_ _F_ 14. The choice of means of financing government functions is made through the mechanism of collective choice.

_T_ 15. Taxes may have harmful effects on incentives to produce, consume, and invest.

_F_ 16. Finance tools tend to be the same regardless of level of government.

_F_ 17. Payroll taxes are a minor financing tool for the federal government. _1^st or 2nd largest._

_T_ 18. Government can provide us with goods and services that we can not easily provide for ourselves or produce through market interaction.

_T_ 19. In a pure market economy, there is no role for government. _stabilization, rules_

_F_ 20. Modern economics bases the study of government activity on a theory of individual behavior. _collective choice_

_T_ 21. United States taxpayers give up more of their income each year to support the activities of government than they do to satisfy their desires for such basic items as food, clothing, and shelter.

Multiple Choice Questions: Choose the best answer.

_e_ 1. Government provision of goods and services requires:
   a) labor.
   b) equipment.
   c) buildings.
   d) land.
   e) all of the above.

_B_ 2. Which of the following is an example of a government good or service?
   a) food.
   b) parks.
   c) clothing.
   d) automobiles.

_C_ 3. Government goods and services:
   a) are made available to buyers on the basis of willingness to pay.
   b) are distributed through the market.
   c) are allocated through non-market rationing.
   d) are only available to taxpayers and their families.

_D_ 4. Government purchases for consumption and investment:
   a) result in a redistribution of economic resources among individual citizens.
   b) only occur at the federal level.
   c) only occur at the local level.
   d) require productive resources to be diverted from private to government use.

5. Which of the following is not a transfer payment by government?
   a) Social Security.
   b) road construction.
   c) unemployment compensation.
   d) payments to disabled veterans.

6. It is virtually impossible to measure government output because:
   a) government is so large.
   b) we need to account for the great inefficiencies in government production.
   c) government goods are sold in private markets.
   d) government goods are generally not sold or produced in easily measurable units.

7. The category of government expenditures that absorbs the largest portion of federal revenues is:
   a) social security and income support.
   b) national defense.
   c) education.
   d) health and hospitals.

8. State and local governments spend the largest portion of their funds on:
   a) transportation.
   b) health and hospitals.
   c) education.
   d) income support, social security, and welfare.

9. Taxes:
   a) represent compulsory payments.
   b) are the principal means of financing government expenditures.
   c) paid do not necessarily bear any direct relationship to the benefits received from government goods and services.
   d) all of the above.

10. The federal government's leading source of revenue is:
    a) borrowing.
    b) personal income taxes.
    c) corporation income taxes.
    d) excise taxes.
    e) payroll taxes.

11. State and local governments receive the largest amount of revenue from:
    a) personal income taxes.
    b) property taxes.
    c) sales taxes.
    d) federal grants.
    e) corporation income taxes.

12. Among the economic functions of government is:
    a) the establishment of property rights to use resources.
    b) the enforcement of contracts.
    c) redistribution of income and economic opportunity.
    d) stabilization of economic fluctuations.
    e) all of the above.

13. The *social compact:*
    a) refers to the willing submission of individuals to the authority of government.
    b) refers to the document signed on the Mayflower in 1620.
    c) defines the collective choice mechanism used for government decisions.
    d) is no longer important.

14. The United States economy is:
    a) a market economy.
    b) a mixed economy.
    c) a command economy.
    d) all of the above.
    e) none of the above.

15. Public finance:
    a) studies the alternative means of financing government activities.
    b) develops principles for understanding the economic role of government.
    c) is interested in government's effect on the well-being of citizens.
    d) all of the above.

Short Answer Questions: Answer in the space provided.

1. Government has many different means of financing its activities. Try to list all the different ways in which you contribute to the financing of government. Try to separate your payments out by the level of government receiving them. Do not forget to include payments for government services (for example, marriage license fees). Try to estimate the amount paid via each financing tool.

2. What is the most important service you receive from government? How much would you be willing to pay for this service if you purchased it in a market? How does this compare with your estimated payment to the government for the service? Why are you likely to overestimate this payment to the government?

3. How does the operation of your school relate to the operation of government? Be sure to define the explicit relations between the school and the government, the parallels in provision of goods and services, the financing mechanisms used by the school, and the mechanisms by which resources are allocated and distributed within the school.

SKETCH ANSWERS TO CHAPTER 1

Issue in Brief:

1. Federal spending for social security pensions, medicare, and medicaid benefit people over the age of 65. As of 1996 Social Security was the largest component of federal spending accounting for 22.5% of all spending. Medicare and Medicaid account for 20% of federal spending. Therefore a very large portion of the federal budget—over 40%—currently benefits people over the age of 65.

2. As the population ages the government will spend more and more on pensions and health benefits for the elderly. These programs are likely to absorb more than half the federal budget by the mid 21st century unless changes are made in the benefit programs.

3. Aging of the population is likely to result either in higher tax rates on the working population, cuts in spending for other programs, or ballooning federal budget deficits later in the 21st century.

True/False:

1. T
2. T
3. F   They are usually distributed through non-market rationing.
4. F   They are generally mixed economies.
5. F   They are government purchases
6. F   Federal expenditures are larger.
7. F   Account for a lower proportion of GDP.
8. T
9. T
10. F   Recently federal grants have decreased.
11. F   Social security is the largest category.
12. T
13. F   Think about the large number of government transfer programs.
14. T
15. T
16. F   Finance tools vary between levels of government.
17. F   Payroll taxes are a very important revenue tool of the federal government.
18. T
19. F   The government still has the important role of enforcing property rights and contracts in a pure market economy.
20. T
21. T

Multiple Choice:

1.	e	5.	b	9.	d	13.	a
2.	b	6.	d	10.	b	14.	b
3.	c	7.	a	11.	c	15.	d
4.	d	8.	c	12.	e		

Short Answer:

1. Common payments would be sales taxes, product excise taxes (for example, long-distance phone service, tires), social security taxes, income taxes, recreation use fees (pools, golf courses, national parks).

2. The payment is likely to be overestimated due to the many "hidden" services provided by government and paid for by your taxes.

3. Think about the services provided by the school, the relationship of your tuition and fees to those services, and the community aspects of the campus existence.

Chapter Recap: You should now be able to answer the following questions:

1. How is public finance defined?

2. How has the relative size of government in the United States changed during the last century?

3. Describe the relationship between government, political institutions, and collective choice as they relate to public finance.

4. How does non-market provision of goods and services differ from market provision?

5. How is the opportunity cost of government activity measured?

6. Draw a circular flow diagram for a mixed economy.

7. What is the difference between an exhaustive expenditure and a transfer payment?

8. Describe the structure of government revenues and expenditures in the United States.

9. Carefully outline the basic reasons for governmental activity.

APPENDIX TO CHAPTER 1

Tools of Microeconomic Analysis

Appendix Objectives: After reading and working through this appendix, you should understand the following:

1. The basic tools of microeconomic analysis used in public finance.

2. The basis for public finance as an applied microeconomic field.

APPENDIX REVIEW QUESTIONS

Short Answer Questions: Answer in the space provided.

1. What are the basic assumptions underlying indifference curve analysis?

2. What pieces of information are required in order to draw a budget constraint?

3. Explain how changes in income and changes in prices affect the budget constraint.

4. Carefully state the law of demand.

5. What is consumer surplus?

6. A profit-maximizing firm produces until which two variables are equated?

7. In the short run, a firm will choose to produce as long as
   _____ .

8. A perfectly competitive industry is in long-run competitive equilibrium only when economic profits are _____ .

9. Be sure that you can identify and use all highlighted terms in the appendix. Use the space below to make notes as you work through the appendix's basic microeconomic review.

SKETCH ANSWERS TO APPENDIX REVIEW QUESTIONS

Short Answer Questions:

1. Completeness (all market baskets can be ranked), transitivity, "more is better", and diminishing marginal rate of substitution.

2. Consumer income and the prices of the goods in the economy.

3. Changes in income shift the budget line in (for a drop in income) or out (for an increase in income) parallel to itself without changing its slope. Changes in relative prices change the slope of the budget line.

4. There is an inverse relationship between product price and quantity demanded.

5. Consumer surplus is the total benefit of a given amount of a good less the value of money given up to obtain that quantity.

6. Marginal cost and marginal revenue.

7. Price exceeds average variable cost.

8. Zero.

CHAPTER 2

Efficiency, Markets, and Governments

Chapter Objectives: After reading and working through this chapter, you should understand:

1. The realm of positive and normative economic analysis.

2. The nature and use of the efficiency criterion.

3. The nature of a perfectly competitive market system and its role in the allocation of resources.

4. The conditions under which markets and prices fail to efficiently allocate resources.

5. The idea that government intervention in markets can lead to losses in efficiency.

6. The trade-off between equity and efficiency.

Chapter Summary:

1. This chapter is probably the most important foundational chapter in the text. It provides a clear look at the analytical basis of public finance, a framework used throughout the rest of the book to evaluate the impact of government resource use on the economic well-being of citizens.

2. Positive economics involves the use of techniques of analysis designed to establish cause and effect relationships among economic variables. Such analysis is descriptive in the sense that value judgments regarding what is good or bad or what should be accomplished are avoided. On the other hand, normative economics is designed to make recommendations as to what should be accomplished. These recommendations are made through evaluation of alternative courses of action based upon criteria established by a set of underlying values. Hence, normative economics is not objective and is intimately dependent on the set of underlying values. In public finance, these values typically embody an individualistic ethic. Both the positive and

normative approaches are useful, and there are elements of dependence between the two approaches.

3. Efficiency (a normative criterion) is satisfied when resources are allocated in such a way as to make it impossible through reallocation to increase the well-being of any one person without reducing the well-being of any other person. This is also referred to as the criterion of Pareto optimality.

4. Marginal social benefit of a good refers to the extra benefit obtained by making one more unit of the good available over any given time period. The marginal social benefit can be measured by the maximum amount of money persons would be willing to pay to obtain the extra unit of the good or service. Marginal social cost is the minimum amount of money that is required to compensate the owners of inputs used in producing a good for making an extra unit of the good available.

5. The marginal conditions for efficient resource allocation require the allocation of resources to production of each good over each time period such that marginal social benefit (MSB) is equated to marginal social cost (MSC).

6. A complete system of perfectly competitive markets with no spillover costs or benefits associated with any good will satisfy the efficiency criterion when each market is in equilibrium.

7. Competitive markets will fail to achieve efficiency when prices do not fully reflect marginal social cost and/or marginal social benefit. This often occurs because of the nature of certain goods, which makes them difficult to package and trade easily in markets. It also occurs in the presence of market power.

8. Government intervention in the market can be used to restore efficiency. However, government intervention often introduces its own distortions which may prevent attainment of efficiency. Taxes and subsidies can affect economic incentives and cause losses in net benefits.

9. Market failure to provide all goods in efficient amounts often results in demands for government action. Sources of market failure include: monopoly power, spillover effects of market transactions, lack of a market for a good whose MSB > MSC, incomplete information, economic fluctuations, and inequitable market outcomes. Government activities are directed at these market failures.

10. Normative criteria often conflict. One common conflict is that between efficiency and equity, that is, the fairness of the outcome. This is an especially difficult conflict because persons differ in their ideas about fairness. Nevertheless, we observe the persistence of inefficient government policies and functions due to organized political action designed to defeat improvements in efficiency on the basis of some notion of equity.

11. The trade-off between improvements in efficiency and changes in the distribution of individual well-being can be illustrated with a utility-possibility curve. This curve gives the maximum attainable level of utility for any one individual, given the utility of all other individuals in the economy and their tastes, resource availability, and technology.

12. The trick in devising efficient policies is to make maximization of net personal benefits coincide with maximization of net social benefit.

Issue in Brief: Hard Heads, Soft Hearts

Alan Blinder's 1987 book, *Hard Heads, Soft Hearts*, was aptly subtitled *Tough-Minded Economics for a Just Society*. In his book, Blinder accuses traditional Republican policies of being hardheaded and hard-hearted, that is "long on rational economic calculation but short on compassion." On the other hand, he accuses traditional Democratic policies of being soft hearted and soft headed, that is "sympathy for the underdog is in abundant supply...,[b]ut... the requisite economic calculations and respect for markets [are] too often lacking." Hard Heads, Soft Hearts provides an interesting look at the way that economic advice is used in policymaking. Watch for a follow-up book now that Blinder has experienced policymaking first hand as a member of President Clinton's Council of Economic Advisers and then as Vice Chair of the Federal Reserve Board of Governors. For further information see: Alan S. Blinder, *Hard Heads, Soft Hearts*, Addison-Wesley, 1987.

Questions for Discussion:

1. To what concept discussed in Chapter 2 does the notion of "hardheaded" policy refer?

2. What about the notion of "soft hearted" policy?

3. Blinder asserts that economists are listened to most on the topics where they know the least and are in the greatest disagreement, while they are listened to least on topics where economists know the most and are in substantial agreement. How do you evaluate his assertion?

CHAPTER REVIEW QUESTIONS

True/False Questions: If false, explain how to correct the statement to make it true.

F 1. Normative and positive economics are two unrelated approaches to economic analysis. *Dependent & interrelated*

2. Barriers to mutually gainful trade prevent achievement of efficiency.

_T_   3. Paternalism suggests that not all mutually gainful trades should be allowed.

_F_   4. Generally, marginal social benefit equals marginal private benefit.

_T_   5. In computing marginal social costs, it is assumed that output is produced at minimum possible cost.

_F_ _T_   6. Total social benefit is calculated by taking the slope of the marginal social benefit curve at any point. $MSB = slope\ TSB$

_F_ _T_   7. As long as MSB > MSC, Pareto efficiency is achieved. $MSB = MSC$

_T_   8. When the marginal condition for efficient resource allocation is satisfied, the marginal net benefit is zero.

_F_ _T_   9. The efficiency criterion maximizes total social benefit.   Net Social Benefit

_T_   10. Under perfect competition, the MSC curve is the market supply curve.

_T_   11. Air pollution caused by the production of a good is likely to prevent the attainment of Pareto efficiency in the market for that good.

_F_   12. Government intervention in a market system always increases the ability of the system to attain efficiency.

_F_   13. Equity is generally a complementary normative criterion to efficiency.

_F_   14. The criterion of equity is universal in definition.

_T_   15. The trade-off between efficiency and equity can be illustrated with a utility-possibility curve.

_T_   16. Inefficient points in the utility-possibility model may be preferred to efficient points.

_F_   17. The market system receives high marks on the basis of equity criteria.

_F_   18. Individuals are primarily concerned with net social benefit as they make their decisions.

_F_ _T_   19. The efficiency criterion is widely applicable for public policy decisions.   few, & quickly exhausted

_F_   20. Application of the compensation criteria increases the number of allocative changes which will be approved.

_T_   21. Market failure provides a justification for government intervention/action.

Multiple Choice Questions: Choose the best answer.

B   1. Positive economics:
   a) is dependent upon underlying values.
   b) establishes cause and effect relationships.
   c) allows one a method for choosing between conflicting policies.
   ~~d)~~ involves much subjectivity.

E   2. Normative economics, as used in public finance:
   a) embodies an individualistic ethic.
   b) is dependent upon underlying values.
   c) is complementary to positive analysis.
   d) formulates recommendations about what should be.
   e) all of the above.

B *A*   3. If resources are used over a given period of time in such a way as to make it impossible to increase any one person's well-being without reducing the well-being of any other person:
   a) there is no reason to change the economy's allocation of resources.
   b) the efficiency criterion has been satisfied.
   ~~c)~~ the distribution of resources is equitable.
   ~~d)~~ total social benefit is maximized.

C *D*   4. Which of the following statements is false?
   a) The opportunity cost of any change in resource allocation is the forgone satisfaction of not making that change.
   b) Constraints that prevent resources being used and traded in such a way as to allow mutual gains will prevent achievement of efficiency.
   ~~c)~~ When efficiency is attained, mutual gains from reallocating resources in productive use or through trade will be positive.
   d) The criterion of efficiency is based on an underlying individualistic ethic.

A   5. "The value of all resources necessary to make a given amount of the good available in a given time period" refers to which of the following concepts?
   a) total social cost.
   b) marginal social cost.
   ~~c)~~ total private cost.
   ~~d)~~ marginal private cost.

D   6. Marginal net benefit is equal to:
   a) MSB – MPB.
   b) MSB + MPB.
   c) MSB + MPC.
   d) MSB – MSC.
   e) MPB – MSC.

7. When MSB = MSC, which of the following is maximized?
    a) marginal social benefit.
    b) total social benefit.
    c) marginal social cost.
    d) net private benefit.
    e) net social benefit.

8. Producing until TSB = TSC:
    a) would maximize total net social benefit.
    b) would involve a lower level of production than producing until MSB = MSC.
    c) would involve a higher level of production than producing until MSB = MSC.
    d) would result in a negative net social benefit.

9. Which of the following is a defining characteristic of a perfectly competitive market system?
    a) private ownership of resources.
    b) full and free information.
    c) mobility of resources.
    d) dispersed economic power.
    e) all of the above.

10. If consumers are the only recipients of benefits when a good is sold, the MSB curve:
    a) is upward sloping.
    b) is the market supply curve.
    c) can not be interpreted.
    d) is the market demand curve.

11. The basic problem that causes inefficiency in competitive markets is:
    a) changes in technology.
    b) prices do not always fully reflect the marginal social benefits or marginal social costs of output.
    c) government-induced distortions that cause marginal social cost to exceed marginal social benefit.
    d) informational asymmetries.
    e) the existence of market power.

12. For a monopolist:
    a) P = MSB < MSC.
    b) P = MSB = MSC.
    c) P = MSB > MSC.
    d) P = MSC > MSB.
    e) P = MSC < MSB.

13. When MSB > MSC for a given good or service:
    a) more than the efficient amount is being produced.
    b) less than the efficient amount is being produced.
    c) the efficient amount is being produced.
    d) the efficient amount may be greater or smaller than this amount.

14. The utility possibility curve gives the maximum attainable level of well-being for any one individual given:
    a) the utility level of other individuals in the economy.
    b) resource availability.
    c) the individual's tastes and preferences.
    d) technology.
    e) all of the above.

15. Points outside the utility possibility frontier are:
    a) inefficient.
    b) points of individual satiation.
    c) consumer equilibrium points.
    d) unattainable.

16. Points inside the utility possibility frontier are:
    a) inefficient.
    b) points of individual satiation.
    c) consumer equilibrium points.
    d) unattainable.

17. Movement from an inefficient allocation to an efficient allocation in the utility-possibility model will:
    a) increase the utility of all individuals in the model.
    b) decrease the utility of all individuals in the model.
    c) increase the utility of a least one individual, but cannot decrease the utility of any individual.
    d) increase the utility of at least one individual, but may decrease the level of utility of another person.

18. In evaluating public policy, we must remember that individuals are primarily concerned with:
    a) total social benefit.
    b) net social benefit.
    c) total private benefit.
    d) net private benefit.

19. Under the Kaldor-Hicks criterion,
    a) equity is given primary weight.
    b) efficiency is achieved in an unfettered market.
    c) the efficiency of a change is independent of whether losers are actually compensated for their losses.
    d) the efficiency of a change is dependent upon any losers being compensated for their losses.

20. Which of the following is an example of market failure?
    a) a drought-related food shortage.
    b) the existence of a cocaine market.
    c) air pollution in urban areas.
    d) stockpiles of cheese and milk in government warehouses.

21. Economic stabilization is not studied as a part of modern public finance because:
    a) public finance focuses on the microeconomic aspects of government activity and finance.
    b) stabilization is not a legitimate role for the government.
    c) stabilization policies have a poor track record.
    d) public finance is only concerned with taxes and expenditures.

Short Answer Questions: Answer in the space provided.

1. Normative analysis is intimately dependent upon underlying values. Try to make a list of some of the fundamental values which underlie your own normative decisions. (Hint: Begin with trying to define your personal notion of equity.) How does your underlying set of values affect your position on economic policy issues?

2. "Constraints that prevent resources being used and traded in such a way as to allow mutual gains will prevent achievement of efficiency." Nevertheless, many people argue that not all mutually gainful trades should be allowed. Make a list of government constraints on mutually gainful trades and justify each constraint in terms of criteria other than efficiency. How does your answer to Question 1 affect your evaluation of the desirability of such constraints?

3. List an actual example of each type of market failure discussed in Chapter 2 of your text. What type of government response has taken place in each of these cases?

Problems: Be sure to show your work.

1. Efficiency, Markets, and Monopoly Power

   a) Suppose that the marginal social cost of clothes dryers is given by MSC = 2Q. Further suppose that the monthly demand for hair dryers is given by the equation Q = 40 – P. What is the efficient level of monthly output of clothes dryers?

   b) If clothes dryers are sold in a monopolistic market, graphically show that the monopolist's optimum output will be less than the efficient output. (Note: no calculations are required here.)

c) Given that the marginal revenue for our monopolist can be correctly written as MR = 40 − 2Q, illustrate the loss in efficiency due to monopoly power in this market. What is the dollar value of this loss?

2. Efficiency, Markets, and Incomplete Information A new drug is developed. It is known that this drug reduces joint inflammation like that caused by arthritis. Based upon this knowledge, the drug is placed on the market.

a) Assume that this drug has substantial side effects which are not reported. Illustrate how this example of incomplete information might lead the drug to be consumed in an inefficient amount.

b) How would your answer change if the drug had substantial medicinal properties, instead of side effects, which extended beyond joint inflammation?

SKETCH ANSWERS TO CHAPTER 2

Issue in Brief:

1. "Hardheaded" policy refers to application of the notions of efficiency and the efficiency criterion.

2. "Soft hearted" policy corresponds to application of policy based on the equity criterion.

3. Compare your answer with those of your classmates. As a hint, think about the degree of the differences of opinion that occur between economists on fundamental issues like the law of demand as compared with differences of opinion on issues like monetary and fiscal policy (i.e., on what types of issues do economists tend to agree? disagree?)

True/False:

1. F   The approaches are often dependent and interrelated.
2. T
3. T
4. F   Many things, like spillovers, cause these two measures to diverge.
5. T
6. F   MSB is the slope of TSB.
7. F   MSB = MSC is the required condition.

8. T
9. F   Net social benefit is maximized.
10. T
11. T
12. F   Government intervention may introduce distortions.
13. F   The criteria often conflict.
14. F   The equity criterion is very individualized.
15. T
16. T
17. F   The market system cannot assure an equitable distribution of goods and services or resources.
18. F   Concern is with net private benefit.
19. F   Few public policy changes satisfy the criterion and those that do are quickly exhausted.
20. F   It is only a hypothetical criterion which does not directly influence collective choice.
21. T

Multiple Choice:

1. b	7. e	13. b	19. c
2. e	8. c	14. e	20. c
3. b	9. e	15. d	21. a
4. c	10. d	16. a	
5. a	11. b	17. d	
6. d	12. c	18. d	

Short Answer:

1. Think about how your values relate to protection of individual freedom, voluntary contracting, equal opportunity, affirmative action, charity, etc. Try to link your values to your positions regarding public policy. Compare your values with those of classmates, family, fellow members of organizations (for example, churches, fraternal organizations, political parties).

2. Some examples are laws prohibiting drug sales, murder contracts, prostitution. Your values are likely to have much to do with your evaluation of these constraints on trade.

3. Some examples include: AT&T in the 1970s (monopoly power), air pollution by coal-fired plants (spillovers), flood insurance (lack of a market for a good whose MSB > MSC), used-car market (incomplete information), unemployment (economic fluctuations), certain types of poverty (inequitable market outcomes).

Problems:

1.

    a) $2Q = 40 - Q$
         $3Q = 40$
         $Q = 40/3$

    b)

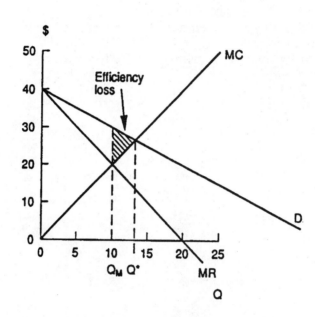

    c) $2Q = 40 - 2Q$
        $4Q = 40$
        $Q = 10$
        $MC = 20$
        $P = 30$

        efficiency loss is given by:
        $.5(30 - 20)(13.33 - 10) = 50/3$.

2.

a)

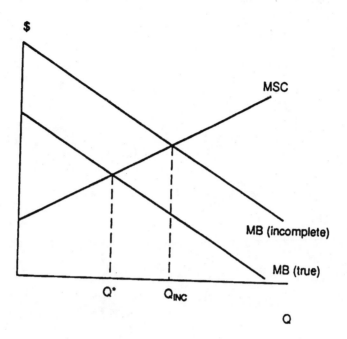

b)

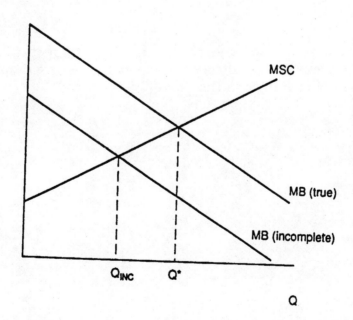

Chapter Recap: You should now be able to answer the following questions:

1. Carefully define and distinguish positive and normative economic analysis.

2. What is meant by the efficiency criterion? Describe its use.

3. What are the assumptions underlying a perfectly competitive market system? What implications does satisfaction of these assumptions have for the allocation of resources in the economy?

4. Under what conditions do markets and prices fail to efficiently allocate resources?

5. Briefly describe how government intervention in markets can lead to efficiency losses.

6. Carefully describe the tradeoff between equity and efficiency. (A utility-possibility frontier may aid in elucidating your answer.)

APPENDIX TO CHAPTER 2

WELFARE ECONOMICS

Appendix Objectives: After reading and working your way through this appendix, you should understand:

1. The graphical and algebraic development of productive and Pareto efficiency.

2. The attainment of productive and Pareto efficiency in a pure market economy.

3. The issue of income distribution in a pure market economy.

4. The impact of market power on the attainment of efficiency.

APPENDIX REVIEW QUESTIONS

Short Answer Questions: Answer in the space provided.

1. What information does a production function provide?

2. What defines productive efficiency?

3. In an Edgeworth box diagram, how are points of productive efficiency characterized?

4. What is the algebraic condition that corresponds to your answer to Question 3?

5. In a conventional production-possibility model, how many points of productive efficiency are there?

6. When deriving the conditions for Pareto efficiency, what goes inside the Edgeworth box?

7. What is the algebraic condition for Pareto efficiency? (Assume a two-good, for example, C and F; and a two-consumer, for example, A and B, world.)

8. How do normative economists attempt to rank efficient outcomes?

9. What is the general condition for minimizing the cost of production of any output?

10. What is the major determinant of the particular efficient resource allocation achieved by a market economy?

11. Use the space below to make notes as you work through the appendix's discussion of welfare economics.

SKETCH ANSWERS TO APPENDIX REVIEW QUESTIONS

Short Answer Questions:

1. The technological conditions under which inputs are converted to output. The production function gives the maximum attainable output from any input combination.

2. Productive efficiency exists if it is not possible to reallocate alternative uses in such a manner as to increase the output of any one good without reducing the output of some alternative good.

3. Points of tangency between the isoquants of the goods in question.

4. $MRTS_{LK}^A = MRTS_{LK}^B$

5. Since all points on the frontier are efficient, there are an infinite number of productively efficient points.

6. Utility functions are plotted through the use of indifference curves.

7. $MRS_{CF}^A = MRS_{CF}^B$

8. Through development and use of a social welfare function.

9. The marginal rate of technical substitution must be equated to the ratio input prices.

10. The initial income distribution between the consumers.

CHAPTER 3

Externalities and Government Policy

Chapter Objectives: After reading and working your way through this chapter, you should understand:

1. What an externality is.

2. What the different types of externalities are.

3. What effects externalities have on the ability of markets to achieve economic efficiency.

4. What kinds of public and private responses can be made to deal with the problems created by externalities.

5. The Coase Theorem and its significance.

6. What internalizing an externality means.

7. The economic effects of both command and control methods and market-based methods of environmental protection.

8. What the general theory of second best is and how it can be applied.

Chapter Summary:

1. This chapter concentrates on the correction of inefficiencies in the market created by externalities.

2. Markets operating under conditions of perfect competition produce efficient outcomes. Any violation of the assumptions of the perfectly competitive market model threatens the ability of unfettered markets to achieve an efficient outcome. Most commonly, violation of the competitive assumptions leads to a situation in which market prices do not fully reflect the marginal social benefits or marginal social costs of economic activity. Externalities represent such a violation.

3. *Externalities*, also known as spillover effects, refer to the effects that economic activities (for example, consumption, production, exchange) have on the well-being (that is, utility for consumers, profits for producers) of economic agents not directly involved in the activity in question, that is, third parties. More precisely, externalities represent benefits or costs of market transactions that are not reflected in prices. That is, market prices do not accurately reflect either all the marginal social benefit or all the marginal social cost of traded items when there is an externality.

4. As long as the spillover benefits or spillover costs are reflected in market prices, as is the case when changes in market demand or supply induced by the actions of a subset of consumers or producers affect the market price for all economic agents, there are no adverse effects on economic efficiency. Some economists refer to these spillovers as *pecuniary externalities*. Pecuniary externalities merely result in changes in real income of buyers and sellers.

5. Unfettered, economic agents will always act so as to equate their marginal private benefit (MPB) with their marginal private cost (MPC). *Real externalities* refer to costs or benefits not reflected in market prices. In the presence of real externalities (from now on, unless specified, we will assume that all externalities discussed are real externalities), setting MPB = MPC is not equivalent to equating marginal social benefit (MSB) and marginal social cost (MSC). If MSB is not equal to MSC, then we fail to reach economic efficiency.

6. The party whose activity creates the externality is often called the emitter and the party whose economic activity is affected by the externality is often called the receptor. Often the nature of externality producing activities is such that the distinction between emitters and receptors is unclear.

7. Externalities may take the form of either spillover benefits or spillover costs and are called positive or negative externalities depending upon which of these forms they take. Externalities arise because the property rights of some resource users are not considered in the market by buyers and/or sellers of products.

8. Economic activities which create negative externalities are overengaged in within unfettered markets. When there is a negative externality, the price of a good or service does not reflect the full MSC of resources allocated to its production. Neither buyers nor sellers consider the costs imposed on third parties. *Marginal external cost* (MEC) is the extra cost to third parties resulting from production of another unit of a good or service and is not fully reflected in the price of the good.

9. With a positive externality, prices do not fully reflect the marginal social benefit of a good or service. *Marginal external benefit* (MEB) is the additional benefit accruing to third parties. Since economic agents base their decisions

on marginal private benefit, positive externalities result in an inefficiently low amount of the economic activity which produces the spillover benefits.

10. Numerous methods of dealing with externalities are available, methods which are based in both private actions and public intervention. *Internalization of an externality* occurs when the MPB or MPC of goods or services are adjusted so that the economic actors consider the true social benefit and social cost of their economic activities as they make their marginal decisions, allowing the efficient level of the externality-producing activity to be attained through the operation of the market.

11. Internalizing an externality can be accomplished through several of the methods available for dealing with externalities. All require clear identification of the individual economic actors involved in the externality and measurement of the monetary value of the marginal external benefits or costs. In general, internalization leads to income redistribution effects which must be weighed against the efficiency gains produced by internalization.

12. *Corrective taxes and subsidies*, also known as Pigouvian taxes, are perhaps the most theoretically straightforward of the publicly based methods of internalization. They are designed to alter the marginal private cost or the marginal private benefit of a good or service so that the economic agents act as if they were accounting for the full costs/benefits of their spillover producing activity.

13. In special circumstances, the internalization of an externality does not require outside intervention in the competitive market. In the absence of transactions costs, externalities involving small numbers of identifiable economic actors (that is, small-number externalities) can be internalized through bargaining by the involved economic agents if the property rights to the involved economic resources are clearly established. *The Coase Theorem* states that merely through the establishment of property rights to use resources, externalities may be internalized through bargaining, regardless of who is assigned the property rights.

14. Other ways government can intervene in the market to alleviate the effects of externalities include such things as emission standards (legally established limits on the amount of "pollution" that can be emitted by a firm), pollution permits (a license or permit to emit a certain quantity of effluent), pollution standards, and the recent use of pollution "bubbles," with corresponding provisions for offsets and the banking of pollution rights. Except in the case of pollution permits, which are auctioned in a free market and auctioned in the precise efficient quantity, these alternative alleviation techniques do not internalize externalities, per se. However, an amount of "pollution" equal to the efficient amount may nevertheless result from these types of non-market constraints.

15. *Command-and-control-regulation* is a system of rules established by government authorities that requires all emitters to meet strict emissions standards for sources of pollution and requires the use of specific pollution-control devices.

16. In general, the efficient level of pollution/externality is the amount of total external cost/benefit which corresponds to that level of the externality producing activity where MSC = MSB. This is normally a nonzero level of activity, vividly suggesting that it is generally not efficient to eliminate an activity producing a negative externality. Rather, efficiency argues for abatement of activities producing negative externalities and enhancement of activities producing positive externalities.

17. When dealing with externalities in imperfectly competitive markets, economists often appeal to the *general theory of second best*. Basically, the theory represents a violation of the typical parent's admonition in that the theory argues that many times two wrongs (inefficiency producing distortions) can add up to a right (economic efficiency). Specifically, introduction of an offsetting distortion can move a market toward the efficient outcome.

Issue in Brief: Trading Pollution Allowances

In November 1994, two large electric utilities, Niagara Mohawk of New York and Arizona Public Service of Arizona, made a first of its kind deal to trade air pollution allowances under provisions in the Clean Air Act of 1990. The agreement represents the first which trades the right to emit one type of pollutant for the right to emit another. Part of the deal also involves using a portion of the proceeds from a tax break generated by the trade to finance reductions of climate warming emissions outside the United States. According to the Environmental Protection Agency, the market-based approach to pollution reduction is already saving rate payers $400 million to $600 million per year. For further information and documentation, see Peter Passell, "For Utilities, New Clean Air Plan," *New York Times*, November 18, 1994, p. C1.

Questions for Discussion:

1. What type of externality is discussed in this issue?

2. Air pollution allowances are a form of what type of pollution control?

3. Do air pollution allowances improve efficiency?

CHAPTER REVIEW QUESTIONS

True/False Questions: If false, explain how to correct the statement to make it true.

T   1. Externalities involve costs or benefits of market transactions which accrue to third parties.

T   2. In an unfettered market, benefits or costs to third parties are not considered by either the buyers or the sellers of an item whose production or use results in an externality.

F   3. In general, externalities are a problem due to their effects on the distribution of income in the economy.

F   4. Negative externalities are those externalities which sellers impose upon third parties through their production activity.

T   5. Positive externalities result in a smaller than efficient level of the economic activity producing the externality.

T   6. Externalities do not cause losses in efficiency if the third party effects occur in the form of market price changes.

F   7. Marginal external cost is the unit cost of correcting for an externality through non-market means.

F   8. An upward sloping total external cost curve indicates that marginal external cost increases with production/use of the good producing a negative externality.

T   9. The MSC of a good must be equated to MSB to attain economic efficiency.

T   10. At market equilibrium, MSB > MSC in the case of an economic activity producing a positive externality.

F   11. Corrective subsidies can be used to internalize negative externalities.

F   12. When a corrective tax is properly implemented, the tax revenue collected will equal the total external cost of the externality it internalizes.

F   13. Internalizing a positive externality increases equilibrium total external benefits above the level that prevailed in the unfettered market equilibrium.

F 14. Internalizing an externality improves the economic well-being of the society.

T 15. Internalizing an externality typically has income redistributive effects.

F 16. Market-based approaches such as corrective taxes or marketable pollution rights can lower the cost of a given amount of emissions reduction.

F 17. Emission standards are an effective internalizing mechanism.

T 18. The Coase Theorem is only operational in the absence of transactions costs.

T 19. It makes no difference to the economic outcome who is assigned property rights under the Coase Theorem.

T 20. The essence of an externality is a dispute over the use of a productive resource.

T 21. Pollution "bubbles" allow firms to exceed emission standards for one or more types of pollutants.

T 22. The main means of dealing with pollution in the United States is government regulation.

F 23. Command-and-control regulation encourages private innovation in pollution control.

Multiple Choice Questions: Choose the best answer.

C 1. Which of the following statements is always accurate?
    a) MSB = MSC.
    b) MPB = MSB + MEB.
    c) MPB = MSB – MEB.
    d) MSC = MPB.
    e) MSC = MPC – MEC.

E 2. In the presence of a real externality,
    a) MSB < MPB.
    b) MSC < MPC.
    c) MSB > MPB.
    d) MSC > MPC.
    e) none of the above.

3. Ace Computer suddenly increases its demand for disk-drive controllers, causing the market price of controllers to increase for all its competitors and suppliers. This is an example of:
   a) a production-induced positive externality.
   b) a consumption-induced negative externality.
   c) a consumption-induced demand externality.
   d) a pecuniary externality.
   e) a real externality.

4. From a social point of view, a good which produces a positive externality when consumed:
   a) will be underconsumed in an unfettered competitive market.
   b) will be overproduced in an unfettered competitive market.
   c) will be overconsumed in an unfettered competitive market.
   d) will be produced at an efficient level in an unfettered competitive market.
   e) none of the above.

5. An upward sloping marginal external cost curve:
   a) is consistent with a positive externality.
   b) rules out the application of the Coase Theorem.
   c) means that the marginal damage of the activity depends on its level.
   d) requires government intervention in order to internalize the externality.
   e) reduces the firm's profits.

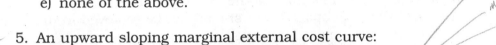

6. The Coase Theorem:
   a) offers private bargaining as a means of internalizing externalities.
   b) can only be applied in the absence of transactions costs.
   c) requires the existence of enforceable property rights.
   d) only applies to small-number externalities.
   e) all of the above.
   f) none of the above.

7. Internalizing a negative externality with a corrective tax will:
   a) eliminate the behavior creating the externality.
   b) requires that compensation be paid to those harmed by the externality.
   c) only occur if the tax revenues are retained by the government.
   d) reduce the level of the economic activity creating the externality.
   e) improve the income distribution of the economy.

8. Externalities require government intervention:
   a) when there is a large number of buyers involved.
   b) when there is a large number of sellers involved.
   c) when property rights are not clearly established.
   d) when transactions costs are non-negligible.
   e) all of the above.

9. Emissions standards:
   a) do not internalize a "pollution-type" externality.
   b) provide an incentive for private innovation in pollution control.
   c) are not effective.
   d) allow the government to strictly control emissions which pollute the environment.

10. Which of the following is the most direct way for government to strictly control the amount of polluting emissions?
   a) a corrective tax.
   b) a corrective subsidy.
   c) the auction of pollution rights.
   d) emission standards.
   e) establishment of property rights.

11. The general theory of second best:
   a) provides the foundation for the Coase Theorem.
   b) argues that monopoly power should not be removed from a market through government intervention.
   c) suggests that efficiency might be achieved by the introduction of an offsetting economic distortion.
   d) suggests that efficiency must sometimes be forgone due to the equity problems its achievement can create.

12. Transaction costs do not include:
   a) driving to the supermarket.
   b) paying an apartment search service to find a rental.
   c) the time invested in writing a sales contract.
   d) the price paid for the good or service.
   e) purchasing cancellation insurance for a nonrefundable airline ticket.

13. A corrective subsidy:
   a) can not be used to internalize a negative externality.
   b) is not as effective as a quota (for example, emission standard) at internalizing an externality.
   c) is crucially dependent upon the tax used to finance it.
   d) requires clear identification of the parties involved in an externality producing activity.
   e) none of the above.

14. A corrective unit tax:
   a) should be set equal to the amount of marginal external cost at the efficient level of output.
   b) will not internalize a negative externality.
   c) should only be used in competitive markets.
   d) has different efficiency effects with respect to different externalities.

15. In general, a corrective tax on a monopolist's output must be _____ the corrective tax that would be necessary to achieve efficiency if the good were produced by a competitive industry.
    a) twice as high as
    b) equal to
    c) less than
    d) greater than

16. Which of the following is currently used in the United States to internalize externalities associated with aircraft noise?
    a) corrective taxes.
    b) corrective subsidies.
    c) pollution permits.
    d) regulation.
    e) all of the above.

Short Answer Questions: Answer in the space provided.

1. Specifically identify five economic activities which produce negative externalities. Try to specify the nature of the external effects, as well as identify the emitters and receptors as clearly as you can. Do you perceive any second best issues?

2. Repeat Question 1 for positive externalities.

3. Which of the externality situations you have described are good candidates for application of the Coase Theorem? Explain.

Problems: Be sure to show your work.

1. *Internalizing an Externality* Go back to Problem 1 at the end of Chapter 3 in your textbook.

   a) Using the information in the problem, explain both graphically and algebraically how this externality could be internalized through the use of a corrective subsidy. (Hint: Think about expressing the marginal external costs as marginal external benefits.)

   b) Compare the efficient outcome which results from your internalization with that which occurs when a corrective tax is used. *Ceteris paribus,* what is the economic difference between these two outcomes? Why might one choose to use the corrective subsidy rather than the corrective tax?

2. *Externalities, Efficiency, and Corrective Taxes*: The supply of coal-powered electricity is given by Qs = 100P, where Qs is the kilowatts supplied each year and P is the price per kilowatt. Demand is described by Qd = 10,000 – 400P, where Qd is the kilowatts demanded each year. Marginal external costs (that is, the costs of acid rain, sooted homes, etc.) increase with electricity output and are given by MEC = .05Qs.

a) Assuming that electricity is sold in a competitive market, what are the equilibrium market price and quantity? What is the efficient annual output of electricity? Show your answers both graphically and algebraically.

$$Qs = 5000P$$
$$Qp = 400,000 - 1000P$$
$$MEQ = 20Qs$$

$$100P =$$

$$100P + 5 = 10000 - 400P$$
$$500P =$$

b) Now, show how a corrective tax can achieve the efficient outcome by internalizing the externality. What will be the appropriate dollar level for the corrective unit tax? How much revenue will the tax raise? How does the efficient level of electricity output vary with the disposition of the tax revenues?

$$100P + 5 = 10,000 - 400P$$
$$500P = 10,005$$
$$= 20.01$$

SKETCH ANSWERS TO CHAPTER 3

Issue in Brief:

1. Air pollution, a negative externality.

2. Pollution rights, a market based approach.

3. Yes, because they serve to internalize externalities.

True/False:

1. T
2. T
3. F   Externalities are generally a problem due to the effect that they have on the market's ability to attain economic efficiency.
4. F   Negative externalities may be emitted by either production or consumption behavior.
5. T
6. T
7. F   Marginal external cost is the extra cost to third parties resulting from an externality-producing activity. It need not equal the unit cost of correcting the externality.
8. F   An upward sloping TEC curve says nothing about the shape of the MEC curve.
9. T
10. T
11. T
12. F   For example, this would not be true if MEC was upward sloping.
13. T
14. F   Internalizing an externality allows the market to achieve the efficient outcome. This says nothing about social well-being, per se.
15. T
16. T
17. F   Emission standards do not internalize externalities.
18. T
19. F   Although resource allocation is not altered by the assignment, the income distribution depends on who is assigned the rights.
20. T
21. T
22. T
23. F   Innovation is discouraged.

Multiple Choice:

1.	c	5.	c	9.	a	13.	d
2.	e	6.	e	10.	c	14.	a
3.	d	7.	d	11.	c	15.	c
4.	a	8.	e	12.	d	16.	d

Short Answer:

1. Check your answers with those of your classmates. Be sure that your external effects flow to parties not directly involved in the economic activity producing the externality and that the external effects are not captured in market prices.

2. Check your answers with those of your classmates. Remember that application of the Coase Theorem requires the establishment and enforcement of property rights and can only be effective with small-number externalities.

Problems:

1. MSB = MPB – MEC is the key equation for conversion from a corrective tax perspective to a corrective subsidy perspective. The demand price and the supply price, as well as the quantity, at the efficient outcome will be the same whether one uses a corrective tax or a corrective subsidy. The economic difference between the use of the two methods is in their effects on the income distribution. *Ceteris paribus*, a corrective tax will reduce the income of emitters and a corrective subsidy will increase the income of receptors. These varying distributional consequences may lead to a preference of one technique over the other. In addition, it may be more feasible to identify and compensate receptors than it is to identify and tax emitters, in which case a corrective subsidy would probably be the preferable route. See Figure 3.2 for graphical analysis of a positive externality.

   CHECK FIGURE: The efficient quantity is 316,667.

2.

a) Market equilibrium price = 20
   Market equilibrium quantity = 2000

   MSC = MPC + MEC
   MSC = Qs/100 + .05Qs = (6/100)Qs
   (since Qs = 100P, Ps = MPC = Qs/100)

   MSB = 25 – (1/400)Qd
   (since Qd = 10,000 – 400P, Pd = MPB = MSB =
   25 – (1/400)Qd)

   For efficiency, MSB = MSC, and in equilibrium we know
   Qd = Qs

   Therefore,
   (6/100)Q = 25 – (1/400)Q
   (25/400)Q = 25
   25Q = 10,000
   Q* = 400
   See Figure 3.1 for graphical analysis of a similar problem.

b) MEC (Q = 400) = 20
   MPC (Q = 400) = 4
   MSC (Q = 400) = 24
   MSB (Q = 400) = 24

   Hence, the corrective tax should be set at $20 per unit and will raise
   $8000 in revenue. The efficient level of electricity output is independent
   of the disposition of the tax revenue. See Figure 3.4 for a graphical
   analysis of a similar problem.

Chapter Recap: You should now be able to answer the following questions:

1. What is an externality?

2. What are the different types of externalities?

3. Describe the effects that externalities have on the ability of an unfettered market to achieve economic efficiency.

4. Describe the kinds of public and private means one might use to deal with externalities. What are the advantages and disadvantages of each of these means?

5. Carefully explain the Coase Theorem and its significance for dealing with externalities.

6. What does it mean to internalize an externality?

7. Compare and contrast the economic effects of command and control methods of environmental protection with those of market based alternatives such as corrective taxes and marketable pollution rights.

8. What is the general theory of second best? Why is it of concern to economists and policymakers who are trying to deal with externalities?

CHAPTER 4

Public Goods

Chapter Objectives: After reading and working through this chapter, you should understand:

1. The nature of a pure public good.

2. The concepts of rivalry in consumption and excludability.

3. The different categories of goods and services and the implications these categories have for the choice of means in making these goods and services available.

4. The character of distribution and production costs as applied to pure public goods.

5. The nature of market demand for a pure public good.

6. The nature of efficiency in the output of pure public goods.

7. The character of voluntary and compulsory finance of pure public goods.

8. The characteristics of Lindahl equilibrium.

9. The nature and implications of the demand-revelation and free-rider problems.

Chapter Summary:

1. This chapter explores the characteristics of goods that are collectively consumed. Alternative methods of supplying such goods are explored and evaluated. The efficiency of collectively sharing the costs of producing goods whose benefits are shared is shown.

2. Market provision of goods with spillover benefits is unlikely to result in the efficient level of output. Hence, government provision of such goods is often considered.

3. *Pure public goods* are characterized by nonrivalry in consumption and are only subject to exclusion at high cost. This suggests the view of public goods as extreme externalities. *Pure private goods* are rival in consumption and their benefits are subject to exclusion. There is a continuum of semipublic goods ranging between pure private goods and pure public goods.

4. The characteristics of rivalry and excludability are independent and do not themselves determine the available or appropriate means of distributing goods and services.

5. The marginal cost of *distributing* a pure public good to additional consumers is zero, while the marginal production cost of public (as well as private) goods is positive.

6. Public goods vary in the range of their benefits. The geographic range of benefits from a public good goes a long way in suggesting the appropriate level of government at which a good might be distributed.

7. The supply of goods and services and the mechanisms of distributing these among individuals reflect collectively agreed-upon institutional arrangements that have emerged in a community. Generalizations about such arrangements are difficult to make. Collective choices determine the form of economic organization to produce and distribute goods and services.

8. *Congestible public goods* are those for which crowding or congestion reduces the benefits to existing consumers when more consumers are accommodated. *Price-excludable public goods* are those whose benefits can be priced, but whose provision results in positive externalities.

9. Political institutions and the market are alternative means of distributing goods and services. Neither institution has exclusive purview over provision of any type of good or service. The choice is based on one or more criteria including efficiency, equity, and paternalistic considerations, as well as the nature of the good or service.

10. The demand for a pure private good involves horizontal summation of individual demand curves, while the demand for a pure public good involves vertical summation of individual demand curves. Horizontal summation adds the quantities demanded across individuals at each given price, while vertical summation adds the individual valuations (marginal benefits) across individuals at each unit of the good.

11. For a pure public good, all consumers must consume the same quantity of the good.

12. Public goods, like all economic activities, are produced at an efficient level when they are produced up to the point where MSB = MSC. This requires that MSC be equated to the *sum* of individual marginal benefits. The

marginal benefit of additional units of a pure public good declines in the same fashion as that of units of pure private goods.

13. In small communities, due to low transaction costs and reduced informational needs, public goods could conceivably be provided in efficient amounts financed through voluntary contributions. Failure to truthfully reveal one's preferences for public goods in this environment may be suboptimal, given the large influence of each member of the community on the government's revenue and on determination of the value of the good or service.

14. A *Lindahl Equilibrium* is reached if all consumers agree on provision of the public good at the efficient level of output, given their cost-share of its finance. All individuals must agree on the amount of the public good desired, the sum of unit contributions for the good must equal the marginal social cost of producing it, and the outcome must be subject to unanimous consent. The individual's equilibrium contributions per unit of the public good are known as Lindahl prices and reflect that consumer's marginal benefit at the equilibrium level of production. Use of a Lindahl scheme requires overcoming the demand revelation problem.

15. The demand revelation problem refers to the failure of an individual to truthfully reveal his/her preferences for a public good. The demand revelation problem is traceable to the use of a revenue-generating mechanism tied to an individual's marginal benefit, as well the the nonrivalrous/nonexcludable nature of a public good.

16. The free-rider problem, related but subtly different than the demand revelation problem, refers to the ability of motivated individuals to consume the full benefits of a public good regardless of their contribution to its production. This problem is most acute when the individual's participation in financing the good is negligible in determining the efficient level of the good (with large numbers of people, each individual is personally responsible for a very small portion of the total bill and total demand), few others free ride (significant free-riding behavior can reduce or eliminate provision of the public good), and the penalties for free-riding are low or nonexistent.

17. Compulsory finance can be used to help overcome the possibility of free-riders consuming goods with collective benefits.

Issue in Brief: Privatizing Public Education

Charter school legislation has been passed on an experimental basis in at least ten states including Michigan, Minnesota, and Massachusetts. In general, such legislation authorizes more than one organization to establish and operate a *public* school in a community (i.e., charter schools can not be elite schools with selective admissions); establishes accountability for chartered schools based on a performance contract; waives application of rules about curriculum, management, and teaching in the chartered school; makes the chartered school a discrete entity that can only be *chosen* by students and educators (i.e., no one will be assigned to teach or go to school there); moves full per pupil state aid with the student as they choose the chartered school; and dovetails teachers into existing state retirement systems and district seniority systems. Most chartered school experiments are part of the broad education reform effort and represent an attempt to investigate the relative effectiveness of education in a deregulated setting with a focus on educational outcomes. For further information, see Joe Nathan, "Chartered Public Schools: A brief history and preliminary lessons," Center for School Change, University of Minnesota, October 1994.

Questions for Discussion:

1. What sorts of regulations still would likely apply to charter schools?

2. What sorts of innovations might you expect a charter school to try?

3. Would you like to have attended a charter school?

4. Primary and secondary education represents an example of what type of good or service?

CHAPTER REVIEW QUESTIONS

True/False: If false, explain how to correct the statement to make it true.

1. A public good refers to a good distributed by government rather than the market.

2. It is efficient for persons to share the costs of producing goods which have collective benefits.

3. Pure private goods are nonrival in consumption.

4. Prices efficiently allocate goods that are rival in consumption.

5. It is generally infeasible to price units of a public good.

6. Goods that are nonrival in consumption are also subject to nonexclusion.

7. Increasing the quantity of a pure public good made available to consumers can be done at zero cost.

8. For a pure public good, all consumers must consume the same quantity of the good.

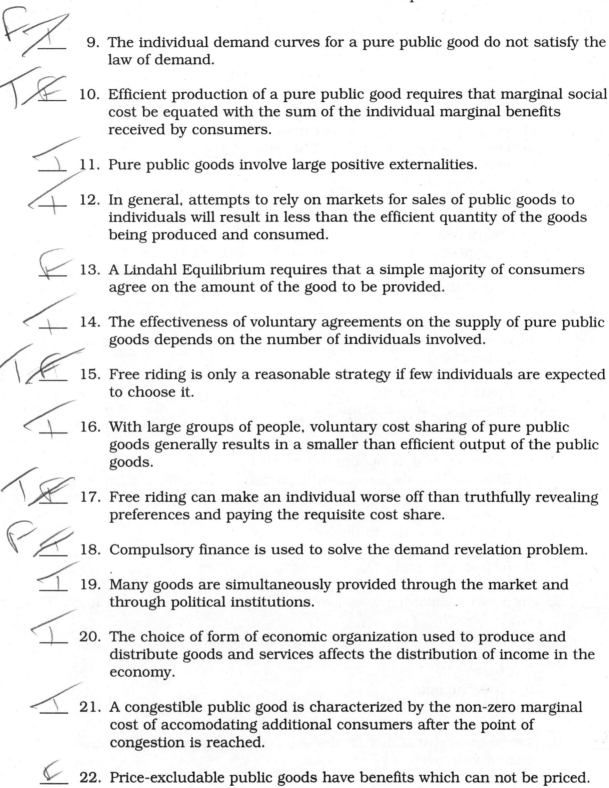

9. The individual demand curves for a pure public good do not satisfy the law of demand.

10. Efficient production of a pure public good requires that marginal social cost be equated with the sum of the individual marginal benefits received by consumers.

11. Pure public goods involve large positive externalities.

12. In general, attempts to rely on markets for sales of public goods to individuals will result in less than the efficient quantity of the goods being produced and consumed.

13. A Lindahl Equilibrium requires that a simple majority of consumers agree on the amount of the good to be provided.

14. The effectiveness of voluntary agreements on the supply of pure public goods depends on the number of individuals involved.

15. Free riding is only a reasonable strategy if few individuals are expected to choose it.

16. With large groups of people, voluntary cost sharing of pure public goods generally results in a smaller than efficient output of the public goods.

17. Free riding can make an individual worse off than truthfully revealing preferences and paying the requisite cost share.

18. Compulsory finance is used to solve the demand revelation problem.

19. Many goods are simultaneously provided through the market and through political institutions.

20. The choice of form of economic organization used to produce and distribute goods and services affects the distribution of income in the economy.

21. A congestible public good is characterized by the non-zero marginal cost of accomodating additional consumers after the point of congestion is reached.

22. Price-excludable public goods have benefits which can not be priced.

Multiple Choice Questions: Choose the best answer.

 1. A pure public good is:
   a) nonrival in consumption and subject to exclusion.
   b) rival in consumption and subject to exclusion.
   c) nonrival in consumption and not subject to exclusion.
   d) nonrival in consumption and not subject to exclusion.
   e) none of the above.

 2. A pure private good is:
   a) nonrival in consumption and subject to exclusion.
   b) rival in consumption and subject to exclusion.
   c) nonrival in consumption and not subject to exclusion.
   d) rival in consumption and not subject to exclusion.
   e) none of the above.

 3. A given quantity of a good can be enjoyed by more than one consumer without decreasing the amounts enjoyed by any consumer. We can say that this good is:
   a) a pure public good.
   b) a pure private good.
   c) nonrival in consumption.
   d) not subject to exclusion.

 4. It is too costly to develop a means of preventing those who refuse to pay from enjoying the benefits of a particular good. We call this property:
   a) nonexclusion.
   b) nonrivalry in consumption.
   c) infeasibility.
   d) the free-rider problem.

5. Which of the following is an example of a good which is nonrival in consumption?
   a) an apple.
   b) a television broadcast.
   c) a book.
   d) a baseball mitt.
   e) a newspaper.

6. The marginal cost of distributing a pure public good to an additional consumer is:
   a) dependent on the good.
   b) negative.
   c) positive.
   d) zero.
   e) indeterminate.

7. Which of the following is not characteristic of a pure public good?
   a) its availability results in widely consumed external benefits.
   b) it is infeasible to price for market distribution.
   c) it is not divisible into units that can be apportioned among consumers.
   d) it is not subject to exclusion.
   e) none of the above.

8. For a pure public good,
   a) consumers can adjust the amounts purchased until the price of the good equals their marginal benefit.
   b) consumers may choose to consume any amount they wish, independent of other consumers' quantity demanded.
   c) market demand is calculated by summing the maximum amounts each individual would pay for each unit of the good.
   d) market demand is calculated by summing the quantity demanded by each individual at each price in a set of possible prices.

9. The efficiency condition for a pure public good is:
   a) MSB = MSC1 + MSC2 + MSC3 +....+ MSCn.
   b) MB = MC.
   c) MSB = MB1 + MB2 + MB3 +....+ MBn = MSC.
   d) MR = P = MC.

10. Sale of a pure public good to individuals in a market is likely to result in:
    a) less than the efficient quantity being produced and sold.
    b) more than the efficient quantity being produced and sold.
    c) production and sale of the efficient quantity.
    d) negative externalities.

11. The marginal social benefit curve for a pure public good is:
    a) upward sloping.
    b) downward sloping.
    c) horizontal.
    d) vertical.

12. In a Lindahl Equilibrium,
    a) each individual desires the identical amount of the public good.
    b) the sum of the amounts contributed per unit equals the marginal social cost of producing the public good.
    c) the outcome is subject to unanimous consent.
    d) all of the above.

13. If persons know that they are required to pay a share of the unit cost of the public good dependent upon their marginal benefits, they have an incentive to understate their true marginal benefits. This is called:
    a) shirking.
    b) the demand revelation problem.
    c) the free-rider problem.
    d) the fiscal finance anomaly.

14. A _____ is a person who seeks to enjoy the benefits of a public good without contributing anything to the cost of financing the amount made available.
    a) free rider.
    b) politician.
    c) shirker.
    b) strategic liar.

15. Pure private goods are supplied through:
    a) the market.
    b) the government.
    c) both the government and the market.
    d) either the government or the market, but not both for the same good.

16. The form of economic organization used to produce and distribute goods and services is determined by:
    a) collective choice.
    b) individual choice.
    c) the market.
    d) government fiat.

17. Congestible public goods:
    a) are nonrival in consumption at all levels.
    b) are characterized by nonexclusion.
    c) are rival in consumption.
    d) can also be price-excludable public goods.

18. An amusement park is:
    a) a pure public good.
    b) a congestible public good.
    c) a price-excludable public good.
    d) both a congestible and a price-excludable public good.

19. The "peace dividend":
    a) will amount to about 6 percent of GNP in the United States.
    b) will be significantly larger for the United States than for the former Soviet Union.
    c) will only be about 1 percent of national output in the United States.
    d) none of the above.

Short Answer Questions: Answer in the space provided.

1. Make a list of goods and services provided by government. What class does each of these goods belong to? Are any of these goods also distributed through the private market? On what basis are these goods provided by government (for example, efficiency, equity, paternalism)?

2. How does the choice of distribution mechanism for goods and services influence the distribution of income in the economy? (Hint: Think of a good which can be provided through market or political institutions and the differences in using these mechanisms.)

Problems: Be sure to show your work.

1. You are given the following marginal benefit curves for three consumers of a good:

Q(A)	MB(A)		Q(B)	MB(B)		Q(C)	MB(C)
1	9		1	7		1	5
2	8		2	6		2	4
3	7		3	5		3	3
4	6		4	4		4	2
5	5		5	3		5	1
6	4						

a) Assuming this good is a pure private good, write out the market demand schedule.

b) Redo part (a) assuming the good is a pure public good instead.

c) If the marginal cost of producing this good is constant at MSC = $15, what will be the efficient level of output if this is a pure public good?

d) What level of production would occur if Person b free rode? Will Person b gain from free riding? Explain.

e) Could any person gain from free riding here? Explain.

2. Is water a public good? Explain.

3. Suppose that the marginal cost of a pure public good decreases as more of it is purchased by a community. What effect will this have on the existence of Lindahl Equilibrium? Why is this an unlikely scenario?

SKETCH ANSWERS TO CHAPTER 4

Issue in Brief:

1. e.g., health and safety, civil rights, and accessibility regulations.

2. e.g., longer school days, reduced certification requirements for teachers, self-paced curricula, emphasis on basic skills curricula, emphasis on mastery of skills rather than traditional graded work.

3. Discuss this with your classmates and families.

4. Education is a price-excludable public good.

True/False:

1. F   A public good is not defined by distribution mechanism.
2. T
3. F   Private goods are rival in consumption.
4. F   Only true if no externalities are present.
5. T
6. F   Goods can be nonrival and excludable.
7. F   Marginal cost of production is positive.
8. T

9.   F   They will still be downward sloping and satisfy the law of demand.
10. T
11. T
12. T
13. F   Unanimity is required.
14. T
15. T
16. T
17. T
18. F   It is generally used to avoid freeriders.
19. T
20. T
21. T
22. F   The benefits can be priced.

Multiple Choice:

1. c	6. d	11. b	16. a
2. b	7. e	12. d	17. d
3. c	8. c	13. b	18. d
4. a	9. c	14. a	19. c
5. b	10. a	15. c	

Short Answer:

1. Compare your answers with those of your classmates. National parks are a congestible public good provided for equity (access to recreational facilities) and paternalistic (forced conservation of wilderness) reasons. Such parks are also provided by the private market in one or more forms (for example, fishing resorts). National parks are also price-excludable public goods as the lines at our more popular campgrounds attest. Similar examples can be given for pure public and pure private goods (for example, national defense and public housing).

2. While the market depends on income from resource endowments to allocate purchasing power, and hence goods and services, the government tends to alter the prevailing income distribution by decoupling the costs and benefits of government services. For example, college education would be distributed differently in the absence of government grant and loan programs which make education at high-priced institutions affordable to those whose market income is inadequate.

Problems:

1.

a)

P	Q
9	1
8	2
7	4
6	6
5	9
4	12

b)

P	Q
21	1
18	2
15	3
12	4
9	5

c) 3 units.

d) Zero units will be produced. Person B will be worse off because no units will be produced without his contribution and positive benefits would result from not free riding with either equal cost shares or cost shares based on marginal valuation of the efficient unit.

e) Yes, Person C could gain from free riding. Persons A and B have a high enough valuation of the public good that one unit will still be produced if C free rides. C gets $5 net benefit from this one unit. This is higher than the net benefit that C gets from telling the truth whether his/her cost share is $5 per unit (equal share scheme) or $3 per unit (marginal benefit scheme).

2. This is a difficult and somewhat ambiguous question. Drinking water is a pure private good. A lake is a congestible public good and/or a price excludable public good. Rain has public good aspects. The answer to this question requires a differentiation between the types of water use and a careful analysis of the characteristics of that good.

3. Not enough revenue will be raised to finance production of the efficient Lindahl quantity. Because the assumptions violate the law of diminishing returns, this is an unlikely scenario.

Chapter Recap: You should now be able to answer the following questions:

1. What features distinguish a pure public good?

2. Compare and contrast the notions of rivalry in consumption and excludability.

3. Carefully contrast the concepts of marginal distribution cost and marginal production cost as they apply to pure public goods.

4. Characterize the market demand for a pure public good.

5. Describe the efficiency conditions for production of a pure public good.

6. Compare and contrast voluntary and compulsory finance of pure public goods.

7. Define and explain the nature and implications of the free-rider and demand-revelation problems.

8. Define the conditions required for Lindahl Equilibrium.

9. Outline the categories within which goods and services can be classified. What are the implications of these categories for the choice of appropriate distributional mechanisms for goods and services?

CHAPTER 5

Public Choice and the Political Process

Chapter Objectives: After reading and working through this chapter, you should understand:

1. How political interaction determines the quantity of goods and services supplied by governments.

2. The concept of political equilibrium and its determinants.

3. The nature of a person's most-preferred political outcome.

4. The costs and benefits of political interaction, including the concepts of government failure and political externalities.

5. The basic costs and benefits of voting and other forms of political activity.

6. The nature and applicability of the median voter public choice model.

7. The concepts of single-peaked and multiple-peaked preferences, as well as their effect on the existence of a unique political equilibrium.

8. The role of political parties in the provision of information, logrolling, and the determination of political equilibrium.

9. The nature and implications of logrolling.

10. The effect of nonvoting behavior on the political equilibrium.

11. The role and effect of special-interest groups in a representative democracy.

12. The role of bureaucracy in the size and management of government.

Chapter Summary:

1. This chapter focuses on public choice and the political process. The theory of public choice studies how decisions to allocate resources and redistribute income are made through a nation's political system.

2. A *public choice* is one made through political interaction of many persons according to established rules. Supply of public goods through political institutions requires agreements on the quantity of the public good and the means of finance. Typically, these agreements are made by simple majority rule votes, involve compulsory means of finance, and thus require those in the minority to abide by the majority vote. However, a variety of collective choice rules can be used to make decisions.

3. A *political equilibrium* is an agreement on the level of production of one or more public goods, given the specified rule for making the collective choice and the distribution of tax shares among individuals. The sum of the tax shares must be sufficient to finance production of the public goods.

4. Individuals are presumed to vote in favor of a proposed public good scheme if they will receive positive net benefits from its passage. That is, as long as the marginal benefit of the good exceeds the person's tax share (their marginal cost of the public good in this framework), the individual will vote for its provision. A rational person's *most-preferred political outcome* is the quantity of the government-supplied good corresponding to the point at which the person's tax share is just equal to the marginal benefit of the good.

5. Voting is the direct means by which collective choices, most primarily the election of political representatives, are made in modern democracies. Like any other economic activity, the decision to vote is made on the basis of comparing the costs and benefits involved in voting, as well as the probability that voting will help achieve the anticipated benefits. Given that there is a high probability that choosing not to vote will *not* affect the outcome of an election, and that the costs of voting are positive, many believe that it is not rational to vote. However, to the extent that voting provides benefits (for example, satisfaction in performing a civic duty) beyond achieving a particular alternative, there may be a rational reason to vote even when one's vote does not affect the outcome.

6. The determinants of political equilibrium include: the collective choice rule, the average and marginal costs of the public good, availability of cost and benefit information to voters, the distribution and structure of tax shares among voters, and the distribution of benefits among voters.

7. *Rational ignorance* is the lack of information about public issues that results because the marginal cost of obtaining information exceeds the apparent marginal benefits of doing so.

8. *Political externalities* are losses in well-being that occur when voters do not obtain their most-preferred outcomes, given their tax shares. *Political transactions costs* measure the value of time, effort, and other resources expended to reach and enforce a collective agreement. Both political externalities and political transaction costs are dependent upon the collective choice rule employed. A trade-off is present in that political externalities are reduced with the requirement of a more definitive majority, while transaction costs are increased due to the greater difficulty in achieving a more definitive majority.

9. *Single-peaked preferences* imply that individuals behave as if there were a unique optimum outcome. *Black's Theorem* states that when all voters have single-peaked preferences, simple majority rule is capable of achieving a unique political equilibrium for a single issue at the median peak for all voters. This move to a unique equilibrium at the median peak is known as the *median voter rule*.

10. *Multiple-peaked preferences* imply that as one moves away from his/her most-preferred alternative he/she becomes worse off at first but eventually becomes better off as movement continues in the same direction. In the presence of multiple-peaked preferences, uniqueness of equilibrium is no longer assured for pairwise voting between multiple alternatives. The ability of a proposal to win under such circumstances is dependent upon the order which alternatives are presented to voters. The failure to have an alternative that can defeat all others regardless of ballot position is a phenomenon called *cycling*, since we can hold repeated elections with no definitive outcome.

11. Though multiple-peaked preferences are inconsistent with declining marginal benefit of public goods, their existence is a very real phenomenon not requiring outlandish assumptions about individual preferences.

12. *Arrow's Impossibility Theorem* states that it is impossible to devise a voting rule that meets a set of conditions which can guarantee a unique political equilibrium for a public choice.

13. *Political parties* allow individuals with similar ideas on issues to group together in some organized form. Political parties also provide a method for voters to identify representatives they desire to pursue their interests in government. The parties themselves play a large informational role in presenting alternatives and their relative merits to voters, both in terms of candidates and policy proposals. Political parties are vote maximizers. As such they engage in much institutional logrolling whereby programs with concentrated benefits and dispersed costs are proposed. Furthermore, the party tries to align itself with the preferences of the median voter so as to maximize its appeal. In the presence of nonvoting, this outcome can differ from the median most-preferred outcome of all citizens.

14. When intensity of preference varies between issues, votes on these issues may be traded to the mutual benefit of those feeling strongly about the issues. This vote trading process is called logrolling. Such vote trading may be conducted through explicit agreement or through the implicit process of pairing unrelated issues into a single election in order to alter chances of passage. Both forms of logrolling are present in our collective choice process. The overall effect of logrolling is subject to debate.

15. Special-interest groups are lobbies that seek to increase government expenditures that benefit their constituents. Unlike political parties, they do not generally present candidates to the voters, although they spend much effort and money on influencing candidates and financing political activities. The most successful interest groups are small so that benefits can be substantial and concentrated relative to the costs imposed on the financing population.

16. Bureaucrats influence the terms of supply of public goods and thus influence the resulting political equilibrium. In the absence of adequate budgeting procedures, the bureaucrats' incentives for power and a maximum budget may lead to a general overextension of the government sector.

Issue in Brief: Line Item Veto

Since 1997 the president of the United States has had the power of the line-item veto. This new power allows a president to veto specific items in a bill passed by Congress rather then either signing or vetoing the entire bill. After the veto of specific items the House and Senate has 30 days to pass a new bill approving the item vetoed. If the president vetoes this new bill his action can be overridden by a vote of two-thirds of the members of the House and Senate.

The line item was used by President Clinton for the first time on August 11, 1997. Since then the constitutionality of the Line Item Veto Act has been challenged in court and it remains to see whether its constitutionality will be unheld by the Supreme Court.

Questions for Discussion:

1. What advantages does a line item veto have over a system that only allows a president to accept or reject an entire bill with a multitude of spending items?

2. What legislative tactic discussed in this chapter would be greatly undermined by a line-item veto?

3. How could the line-item veto reduce government spending?

CHAPTER REVIEW QUESTIONS

True/False Questions: If false, explain how to correct the statement to make it true.

F 1. A public choice is one made through political interaction of many persons always according to majority rule.

F 2. Citizens who vote against an outcome that is enacted need not participate in its finance.

F 3. Information on the costs of producing public goods is generally easy to acquire and disseminate.

F 4. The median voter is the one whose most-preferred outcome is the simple average of the most-preferred outcomes of all those voting.

T 5. When more than two outcomes are possible, majority rule does not ensure that a majority of voters will receive their most-preferred outcome.

F 6. Use of majority rule ensures a unique political equilibrium.

F 7. Multiple-peaked preferences mean that the individual has more than one most-preferred alternative.

T 8. Pairwise elections are those held between any two alternatives from a set of three or more possible alternatives.

T 9. Pairwise elections with multiple-peaked preferences generally result in cycling.

F 10. Cycling can be avoided through altering the order of alternatives.

T 11. With single-peaked preferences for all voters, majority rule leads to the median voter consuming his/her most-preferred alternative.

T F 12. Multiple-peaked preferences are inconsistent with declining marginal benefit of public goods.

F 13. The possibility of multiple-peaked preferences can be ruled out.

T F 14. Incentives to trade votes exist only if there is an asymmetry of gains on the issues involved.

F 15. Logrolling cannot take place in the absence of an agreement among voters.

_____ 16. Logrolling allows for an expression of intensity of preference which is not provided by democratic "one person, one vote" institutions.

_____ 17. If the marginal benefit of a public good declines for all voters, the median most-preferred quantity of the good is always the political equilibrium under majority rule.

_____ 18. Direct participatory democracy does not exist as a form of government today.

_____ 19. The probability of a single voter influencing an election is close to zero when the number of voters is large.

_____ 20. Some nations make voting a legal requirement in order to avoid free-riding by nonvoters.

_____ 21. Very few people vote in nations where voting is not a legal requirement.

_____ 22. Voter turnout in presidential elections in the United States has been declining since 1960.

_____ 23. The net benefit of voting is greatest in the presence of close alternatives.

_____ 24. Political parties serve no useful role in a representative democracy.

_____ 25. Vote-maximizing behavior is a prerequisite to obtaining political power in a democracy.

_____ 26. Political parties attempt to accurately approximate the median most-preferred outcome as they attempt to emerge victorious.

_____ 27. Nonvoting reduces the number of participants in a collective choice decision, but does not affect the final political equilibrium.

_____ 28. Nonvoting may occur both as a result of candidates being too similar and as a result of candidates being too far from the voter's most-preferred positions.

_____ 29. In the presence of alienation nonvoting, political parties tend to move toward the modal rather than median most-preferred outcome.

_____ 30. Bureaucrats fail to efficiently produce public goods.

_____ 31. A bureaucrat seeking to maximize his/her budget may result in overextension of the public sector.

F   32. Special-interest groups have little influence on the political equilibrium in the United States.

T F   33. The most successful special-interest groups are likely to be small relative to the total size of the government's constituency.

T F   34. Political externalities do not exist under unanimous consent.

Multiple Choice Questions: Choose the best answer.

E D   1. Which of the following is not an example of a collective choice rule?
a) simple majority.
b) plurality.
c) unanimous consent.
d) dictatorship.
e) none of the above.

B C   2. In order to avoid a budget surplus or deficit, the sum of the tax shares must equal:
a) marginal cost.
b) average cost.
c) total cost.
d) marginal benefit.

B   3. Which of the following is not a determinant of political equilibrium?
a) the collective choice rule.
b) the extent of spillover benefits.
c) the distribution of benefits among voters.
d) the distribution of tax shares among voters.
e) none of the above.

A B   4. If a public good can be produced under conditions of constant costs, and we wish to have each of the n individuals in a community pay the same tax per unit of the good, each individual's tax share will equal:
a) AC/n.
b) AC.
c) MC.
d) (MC × Q)/n.

C   5. Which of the following collective choice rules will result in the highest proportion of successful proposals?
a) unanimous consent.
b) three-fourth's majority.
c) plurality.
d) simple majority.

C

6. A person prefers large and small public schools to medium-sized schools. This person:
   a) is irrational from an economic perspective.
   b) has single-peaked preferences.
   c) has multiple-peaked preferences.
   d) can not achieve his/her most-preferred outcome.

7. With multiple-peaked preferences,
   a) a unique political equilibrium does not exist.
   b) movements away from the most-preferred point begin by making the individual worse off, but eventually the individual's well-being becomes better off with continued movement in the same direction.
   c) individuals have a most-preferred point.
   d) the property of transitivity does not hold.
   e) all of the above.

8. Empirical evidence suggests that the demand for which of the following services is most elastic with respect to the tax price of the median voter:
   a) local education.
   b) fire protection.   inelastic
   c) police protection.
   d) parks and recreation.

9. Multiple-peaked preferences:
   a) are inconsistent with declining marginal benefits of public goods.
   b) are consistent with rational economic behavior.
   c) were observed during debates about the Vietnam War.
   d) all of the above.

10. Logrolling:
    a) requires differing intensities of preference on issues.
    b) requires symmetry of gains on the issues involved.
    c) is only possible with three or more issues.
    d) results in significant equity losses.

11. Implicit logrolling:
    a) occurs when political interests succeed in pairing two or more issues of strong interest to divergent groups.
    b) requires an explicit agreement.
    c) reduces the chances of passing any single program.
    d) removes dependence on the relative intensity of preference for two divergent issues.

E 12. Arguments against logrolling include:
   a) its overemphasis on intensity of preferences.
   b) its potential use as a means of gaining approval for purely redistributive programs.
   c) its use as a means of gaining benefits which accrue to only small groups of people.
   d) its tendency to extend the size of the public sector.
   e) all of the above except a.

C 13. A voter's most-preferred outcome corresponds to the point at which the marginal benefit of a given quantity of a public good is equal to:
   a) marginal social benefit.
   b) marginal social cost. $= B$ Pvt
   c) the individual's tax share.
   d) average cost.

D 14. Black's Theorem deals with which of the following?
   a) logrolling.
   b) the determinants of political equilibrium.
   c) the decision regarding an appropriate collective choice rule.
   d) the median voter rule.

C 15. Individuals A, B, C, D, and E make up a community. Their most-preferred amounts of the public good to be voted on in a referendum are 1, 3, 4, 8, and 9 units respectively. Assuming single-peaked preferences on the part of all of the individuals and that the marginal benefit of the public good declines for all voters, what will be the political equilibrium for this public good?
   a) indeterminate due to cycling.
   b) 3 units.
   c) 4 units.
   d) 8 units.
   e) 5 units.

A 1
B 3
C 4
D 8
E 9

B 16. In the situation depicted in Question 15, how many voters will be at their most-preferred outcome?
   a) 0.
   b) only Person C.
   c) only Person B.
   d) both Persons B and C.
   e) all voters.

17. The costs of voting include:
    a) reading newspapers to understand the issues and positions of candidates.
    b) gathering information on the costs and benefits of proposed alternatives.
    c) the time and effort necessary to go to the polls.
    d) all of the above.

18. Which of the following does not tend to act as a disincentive to vote?
    a) a large number of voters.
    b) very diverse alternatives.
    c) the electoral college system in states dominated by a single political party.
    d) all of the above are disincentives.

19. Political activity:
    a) may be undertaken for the purpose of logrolling.
    b) is constrained by the "one person, one vote" doctrine.
    c) has the shortcoming that intensity of feeling can not be expressed.
    d) is costless from the point of view of society.

20. Political parties:
    a) have little influence in determining the actual political equilibrium.
    b) rarely include platform proposals appealing to a minority of voters.
    c) are influential in formulating alternatives to be presented to the electorate.
    d) try to discourage vote trading among voters.

21. The median most-preferred outcome Q* for all citizens is such that:
    a) the net benefits of more than half of the voters will be higher under Q* than for any alternative quantity of government goods and services, given tax shares.
    b) is the point at which a political party can maximize the number of votes if the most-preferred outcomes of voters are normally distributed.
    c) will be at a higher level of output than the median most-preferred outcome of voters in the presence of alienation.
    d) will be at a lower level of output than the median most-preferred outcome of voters in the presence of alienation.

22. Which of the following presidential elections illustrates the notion that when political candidates in the United States take extreme positions they lose?
    a) 1960: Kennedy vs. Nixon.
    b) 1964: Johnson vs. Goldwater.
    c) 1968: Nixon vs. Humphrey.
    d) 1976: Carter vs. Ford.

23. When voters choose not to vote because they are alienated,
    a) there is a tendency for political parties to move toward the mode rather than the median of the most-preferred outcomes of citizens.
    b) the median most-preferred outcome can still prevail.
    c) a political equilibrium different from the median most-preferred outcome of all citizens can result if the distribution of most-preferred outcomes is either asymmetric or multinodal.
    d) all of the above.
    e) none of the above.

24. The concept of rational ignorance:
    a) deals with the low probability of economic actors understanding the rational decision-making model.
    b) is fundamental to the question of representative democracy.
    c) says that in the presence of costly information it is often not worth the effort for a voter to analyze a particular issue's costs and benefits.
    d) all of the above.

25. Bureaucracy:
    a) is in charge of implementing collective choices made through political institutions.
    b) influences the actual delivery of services.
    c) influences the political equilibrium through altering the terms of supply of public goods.
    d) is difficult to evaluate on efficiency grounds.
    e) all of the above.

26. Which of the following is not part of Niskanen's analysis of bureaucratic behavior?
    a) the assumption that a bureaucrat's power is correlated with the resources at his/her command.
    b) the argument that bureaucrats will seek funding up to where TSB = TSC.
    c) the conclusion that government projects are underfunded due to informational asymmetry.
    d) the difficulty in managing a bureaucracy for efficiency.

27. According to Hyman, the bureaucrat's utility function includes as an argument:
    a) net benefit to the funding authority.
    b) growth of their budget.
    c) job security.
    d) fringe benefits.
    e) all of the above.

28. Which of the following is an example of a special-interest group?
    a) Republican Party.
    b) National Rifle Association.
    c) National Broadcasting Company.
    d) League of Women Voters.
    e) Consumers' Union.

29. If the tax shares of all voters of government goods and services were adjusted until they equal the marginal benefits received from government output,
    a) political transaction costs would be minimized.
    b) political externalities would be zero.
    c) not all persons would be at their most-preferred outcome.
    d) political equilibrium would be dependent upon the collective-choice voting rule.

Short Answer Questions: Answer in the space provided.

1. Logrolling is a phenomenon in which we all engage in some way or another. Make a list of some instances where you have explicitly or implicitly logrolled. What was the result in terms of your and your fellow logrollers' satisfaction?

2. Try to make a list of items for which you have multiple-peaked preferences. What is the nature of this shape for your preferences?

3. Make a list of five special-interest groups. Carefully list the political activities of each of these groups. Whose interest do these groups pursue? Are these groups effective?

4. Do you regularly vote? How does your individual decision about voting reflect the cost and benefit considerations discussed in Chapter 5?

Problems: Be sure to show your work.
 1. Assume that the marginal cost of a public good is given by MSC = 4Q + 9, and that Persons A, B, and C make up a community and have the following marginal benefit curves for the public good:

$$MB(A) = 10 - Q$$
$$MB(B) = 14 - 2Q$$
$$MB(C) = 15 - 3Q$$

   a) If this good were sold in an unfettered competitive market, how many units would be purchased by our three community members?

   b) What is the efficient level of production of this public good?

c) Would the efficient level of production be achieved by pairwise elections utilizing majority rule, assuming a one-third tax share for each of the individuals?

d) Would the political equilibrium change if Persons A and C now had tax shares of one-fourth and Person B had a tax share of one-half?

e) If the public choice rule were changed to require unanimity for any increase in the provision of a public good, what would be the political equilibrium reached if we begin at 0 units and place successively larger units of the public good before voters?

2. "When voters choose not to vote because they are alienated, there is a tendency for political parties to move toward the mode rather than the median of the most-preferred outcome of citizens."

   a) Carefully make a convincing verbal proof of this statement.

   b) How do the implications of this statement differ depending upon whether the distribution of most-preferred outcomes is symmetric and unimodal or multimodal and asymmetric?

3. Show that, if nonvoting equally affects conservatives and liberals in a situation such as that described in Problem 3 in your textbook, the political equilibrium will be unaffected as compared with the 100 percent voter turnout case.

SKETCH ANSWERS TO CHAPTER 5

Issues in Brief:

1. It would allow the president to approve items in a bill he favors while limiting spending for items for which marginal costs exceed marginal benefits.

2. Logrolling would be undermined.

3. Logrolling tends to increase government spending by allowing programs for which marginal benefits fall short of marginal cost being approved. Exercise of the line-item veto could decrease incentives for such vote trading in Congress thereby decreasing the rate of growth of government spending.

True/False:

1. F   Majority rule is only one possibility.
2. F   All must abide by the results of the collective choice.
3. F   This information is difficult to determine.
4. F   It is the median of preferred outcomes.
5. T
6. F   A unique equilibrium is not ensured.
7. F   It only says that movements away from the most-preferred alternative do not result in a continuous drop in well being.
8. T
9. T
10. F   Cycling occurs because the order of alternatives changes results. Changing the order of alternatives will not allow settlement to equilibrium.
11. T
12. T
13. F   They can not be ruled out.
14. T
15. F   Implicit logrolling takes place without an agreement.
16. T
17. T
18. F   For example, New England town meetings are still held.
19. T
20. T
21. F   Even with recent drops in voting in the United States, more than half of eligible voters turn out.
22. T
23. F   Benefits drop with close alternatives.
24. F   Parties supply candidates and information about alternatives and act as vote-trading brokers, among other things.
25. T
26. T
27. F   This is only true if the distribution of nonvoters is perfectly symmetric about the median.

28. T
29. T
30. F   This is a generalization that can not be supported by objective evidence because output is not easily quantified or valued.
31. T
32. F   They seem to have a profound effect. See the case outlined in the textbook chapter.
33. T
34. T

Multiple Choice:

1.	e	7.	e	13.	c	19.	a	25.	e
2.	b	8.	a	14.	d	20.	c	26.	c
3.	b	9.	d	15.	c	21.	b	27.	e
4.	a	10.	a	16.	b	22.	b	28.	b
5.	c	11.	a	17.	d	23.	d	29.	b
6.	c	12.	e	18.	b	24.	c		

Short Answer:

1. Compare your answer with fellow students. Think about things like taking turns doing things you like with your friends.

2. Each of us has multiple-peaked preferences about one or more things. Try to think about why your preferences take this form on the issues you identify. Compare your answers with those of your classmates.

3. Compare your answers with those of your classmates. One example would be the National Federation for the Blind. They do substantial informational advertising aimed at sighted voters, provide competitive services for the blind, lobby elected representatives, etc. They aggressively represent the interests of the blind in an effective fashion.

4. Carefully reflect on your reasons for voting or not voting. Does any of the information you learned in this chapter alter your view of voting? Compare your feelings with those of your classmates.

Problems:

1.
   a) Zero units will be purchased since MSC > MSB for all quantities for all consumers.
   b) Three units since this is the point where MSC is equal to the sum of the individual marginal benefits.

c) Yes, at three units the net benefits of the individuals are such that Persons A and B, representing a majority in the three person community, would prefer this level to any other level of production. Person C would prefer three units to any other level except for two units. Each individual's total tax share for the 3 units is $17. The individual net benefits are $7, $13, and $10 for Persons A, B, and C.

d) No change except that the majority will now be Persons A and C. A and C will have a total tax share of $12.75, and B will pay $25.50. The net benefits will be $11.25, $4.50, and $14.25 for A, B, and C. Moving an even greater portion of the financing burden to Person B will eventually increase the equilibrium quantity of the public good. As an exercise, try to show this by increasing B's tax share (simultaneously reducing that of A and C).

e) Two units would be the last unit unanimously approved.

2.

a) The key point here is that the mode is the outcome preferred by the largest number of voters. Thus, under the circumstances described, the largest number of voters will be happy and vote when the mode is the outcome proposed. This behavior is therefore consistent with vote maximization.

b) If symmetric and unimodal, the median and mode coincide. If asymmetric and multimodal, they do not.

3. All you have done in this instance is reduce the number of voters. The median will be unchanged and at that point there will still be the requisite majority whose benefits exceed costs and vote in favor of provision.

Chapter Recap: You should now be able to answer the following questions:

1. How does political interaction determine the quantity of goods and services supplied by government?

2. Carefully explain the notion of a political equilibrium. What are its determinants?

3. Carefully explain the notion of an individual's most-preferred political outcome.

4. Carefully describe the costs and benefits of political interaction. Be sure to discuss the concepts of government failure and political externalities in your answer.

5. Identify and evaluate the costs and benefits of political activity including voting.

6. What is the median voter model? Under what circumstances can it be applied?

7. What is the role of political parties in a representative democracy?

8. Define the concepts of single-peaked and multiple-peaked preferences. What effect does the shape of preferences have on the existence of a unique political equilibrium?

9. Describe the nature and implications of logrolling.

10. What effect does nonvoting have on the political equilibrium?

11. What role do interest groups play in a representative democracy? Are they effective?

12. What role does bureaucracy play in the size and management of government?

13. Make a list of collective-choice rules used by government in the United States.

CHAPTER 6

Cost-Benefit Analysis and Government Investments

Chapter Objectives: After reading and working through this chapter, you should understand:

1. The nature and relative merits of program budgeting.

2. The notion of cost-effectiveness analysis and its use as a public sector decision-making tool.

3. The nature and use of cost-benefit analysis for determining the relative merits of government projects over time.

4. The methods and difficulties of measuring the benefits and costs of government investment projects.

5. The notion of the social rate of discount and its role in evaluating the present value of future benefits and costs.

6. The role of cost-benefit analysis in budgeting and the political process.

Chapter Summary:

1. This chapter is primarily concerned with techniques for managing and controlling government expenditures. Efficiency in government requires that the least-cost combinations of inputs be used to achieve any given objective and that the mix of government activities be efficient. Evaluating government projects along these lines can be difficult since governments are not profit-making entities, do not face competition, and make investments over long periods of time that are designed to yield streams of public benefits for years to come. The output of such investments is rarely sold in markets, and thus the return on the investment is difficult to compute.

2. *Program budgeting* is a system of managing government expenditures by comparing the program proposals of all government agencies authorized to achieve similar objectives. Such a system allows trade-offs between programs of agencies with similar missions to be discussed and evaluated.

3. *Cost-effectiveness analysis* is a technique for determining the minimum-cost combination of government programs to achieve a given objective. Cost-effectiveness analysis allows policymakers to see tradeoffs between programs by budgeting together for all agencies whose missions are similar.

4. *Cost-benefit analysis* is a technique for determining the relative merits of alternative government projects over time. Cost-benefit analysis involves enumerating all costs and benefits of the proposed project, evaluating all costs and benefits in dollar terms, discounting future net benefits, and then choosing between those projects with positive net discounted benefits (or benefit-cost ratios greater than 1). The social rate of discount used in the analysis should reflect the opportunity cost of funds invested by the government in the project. Inflation is dealt with through consistent use of either nominal dollars and interest rates or real dollars and interest rates.

5. Although cost-benefit analysis can be a useful tool, it remains difficult to measure the benefits and costs of government goods and services. Issues of valuation and appropriateness hinder many efforts at cost-benefit analysis, as does the ease of discounting the results of the process in favor of politically expedient outcomes.

Issue in Brief: Protectionism and Economic Policy

Most trade restrictions are remarkably unsound when judged by traditional economic policy criteria. Protectionism distorts the allocation of resources in the economy by altering the relative prices of goods, including the relative prices of imports and exports. We also end up paying more for some of the things we buy as a result of trying to keep "cheaper foreign goods" out of our markets. Thus, the standard of living of the average citizen falls. In addition, a trade restriction has redistributive effects, taking from the average consumer and giving to owners and workers in the favored industry or industries. Unfortunately, tariffs and quotas are wasteful ways of redistributing income. The costs of redistribution are typically several times the wages of the protected workers (remembering that typically protection arguments are framed in terms of saving jobs). For example, in *Hard Heads, Soft Hearts*, Blinder refers to a study that estimated that in 1984 consumers paid $750,000 per year for every job saved in the steel industry. Blinder argues that a one time severance of $750,000 per steelworker would likely have been eagerly accepted by the workers and the recurring expenditures associated with protection could have been saved. For further information, see Alan S. Blinder, *Hard Heads, Soft Hearts*, Addison-Wesley, 1987, Chapter 4.

Questions for Discussion:

1. Name some U.S. industries that have been protected in the last twenty or so years.

2. Are the economic effects of a tariff and a quota the same?

CHAPTER REVIEW QUESTIONS

True/False Questions: If false, explain how to correct the statement to make it true.

F   1. Use of government power to redistribute income can be easily evaluated using efficiency criteria.

T   2. The slope of an isoquant is equivalent to the marginal rate of technical substitution between the two products multiplied by -1.

T   3. Cost-effectiveness analysis allows policymakers to see tradeoffs between programs by budgeting together for all agencies whose missions are similar.

F   4. Cost-effectiveness analysis and cost-benefit analysis are just two different names for the same basic analytical technique.

T/F   5. The first step in implementing a cost-effectiveness analysis would be to choose a common objective that alternative government programs can achieve.

F   6. Program budgeting compares budgets involving programs of agencies with different missions. *similar*

T/F   7. Program budgeting has had only limited use in the United States.

F/T   8. Cost-benefit analysis is a relatively new tool developed and used first by the United States Navy. *old – Army Corps of Engineers*

T   9. Since 1981, all new regulations proposed by the federal government must be subjected to cost-benefit analysis.

F   10. Only direct benefits and costs are of concern in cost-benefit analysis.

T/F   11. In enumerating benefits, only real increases in output and welfare are considered.

T   12. When output attributable to a project is sold in an oligopolistic market, market prices must be adjusted to reflect the true marginal social cost and benefit.

___T___ 13. The higher the social rate of discount ceteris paribus the lower the present value of a future stream of benefits.

___F___ 14. The net return earned by savers is generally the same as the net return earned by investors.

___T___ 15. The social rate of discount must take account of the type of private expenditures displaced by the government activity.

___F___ 16. The choice of discount rate affects the net present value of projects, but it does not affect the ranking of alternative projects.

___F___ 17. Inflation creates no problem in cost-benefit analysis.

___F___ 18. Projects will be ranked in the same order whether the criterion used in net discounted benefit or the benefit-cost ratio.

___T___ 19. In practice, cost-benefit analysis is more of an art than a science.

___F___ 20. Cost-benefit analysis makes valuation of human life a straightforward task.

Multiple Choice Questions: Choose the best answer.

___E___ 1. A government budget:
- a) is an informational device.
- b) is a management tool.
- c) represents a plan for government expenditures.
- d) includes information on the means of financing government activity.
- e) all of the above.

___D___ 2. To achieve efficiency, government activities must be undertaken up to the point at which their:
  a) MB = 0.
  b) net benefit is zero.
  c) total benefit is maximized.
  d) MSB = MSC.

___C___ 3. The cost-effective mix of two programs is arrived at by equating their marginal rate of technical substitution with:
  a) marginal social benefit.
  b) marginal social cost.
  c) the ratio of their unit prices.   MRTS = A/B
  d) marginal social utility.

C

4. A combination of government activities producing a distinguishable
   output is called:
   a) a decision unit.
   b) a mission.
   c) a program.
   d) an agency.
   e) a bureau.

B

5. Which of the following statements about cost benefit analysis is false?
   a) Cost-benefit analysis has been used in the United States since
      1900.
   b) Cost-benefit analysis requires little ingenuity.
   c) Use of cost-benefit analysis has as an aim making sure that
      projects whose marginal social costs exceed marginal social benefits
      are not considered for approval.
   d) Cost-benefit analysis represents a practical technique for
      determining the relative merits of alternative government projects
      over time.

D

6. In enumerating benefits,
   a) both direct and indirect benefits must be considered.
   b) only real increases in output and welfare are considered.
   c) extra profits of third parties create a problem for the analyst.
   d) all of the above.

A

7. If the prices of increased agricultural outputs of an irrigation project
   reflect the price supports of United States agricultural policy, in doing
   cost-benefit analysis these prices:
   a) must be adjusted downward to reflect the true marginal social
      benefit of the output.
   b) must be adjusted upward to reflect the true marginal social benefit
      of the output.
   c) need not be adjusted in order to reflect true marginal social benefit
      of the output.
   d) none of the above.

A

8. The present value of $100 received four years from now will be greatest
   using which social rate of discount?
   a) 5 percent.
   b) 7 percent.
   c) 9 percent.
   d) 11 percent.

B

9. If there is a 50-percent tax on corporate profits ceteris paribus,
   a) the gross return to investors will fall short of the net return.
   b) investors and savers will adjust to different interest rates.
   c) the discounted net present value of projects will be reduced.
   d) all of the above.

10. A lower discount rate:
   a) favors projects which yield current net benefits relative to future benefits.
   b) favors projects which yield net benefits in the future relative to current net benefits.
   c) decreases the probability of approving any project.
   d) indicates a higher social opportunity cost of capital.

11. One way of dealing with inflation in performing cost-benefit analysis is to measure benefits and costs over time:
   a) in real terms, inflating all future benefits and costs utilizing the real interest rate.
   b) in real terms, deflating all future benefits and costs utilizing the nominal interest rate.
   c) in nominal terms, inflating all future benefits and costs utilizing the nominal interest rate.
   d) in nominal terms, deflating all future benefits and costs utilizing the nominal interest rate.

12. Using the benefit-cost ratio as the decision criterion, which of the following projects will be most preferred?
   a) Project A which yields $400 in discounted benefits and $200 in discounted costs.
   b) Project B which yields $700 in discounted benefits and $300 in discounted costs.
   c) Project C which yields $1000 in discounted benefits and $2000 in discounted costs.
   d) Project D which yields $5 in discounted benefits and $2 in discounted costs.

13. If the decision criterion in Question 12 were changed to net benefits, which project would be most preferred?
   a) A.
   b) B.
   c) C.
   d) D.

14. In a capital-intensive project:
   a) costs in the early years are likely to be high relative to benefits.
   b) costs in the late years are likely to be high relative to benefits.
   c) costs in the early years are likely to be low relative to benefits.
   d) costs will increase with each year of the project.

15. A cost-benefit analysis of the 55 mph speed limit concluded that:
   a) saving lives is not cost effective.
   b) the benefit-cost ratio of the speed limit regulation exceeds 1.
   c) the benefit-cost ratio of the speed limit regulation is less than 0.5.
   d) the average discounted present value of a life saved is about $1 million.

Short Answer Questions: Answer in the space provided.

1. Most of us use cost-benefit analysis, at least implicitly, to make many of our major decisions. Outline the decision process you used to make a recent major purchase. Try to fit this process into the outline of cost-benefit analysis and perform cost-benefit analysis of the purchase. Is this technique an effective way to evaluate such a purchase? How did you choose an appropriate discount rate?

2. Offer an example of how you have used cost-effectiveness analysis in your daily life. What is the common goal you are trying to achieve? What alternative ways of achieving this common goal are, or were, considered?

3. Your textbook suggests that the effects of a given project on the distribution of income can be built into cost-benefit analysis by weighting costs or benefits according to whom or where they accrue. Returning again to the normative values we have asked you to clarify in this study guide, how would you weight and disaggregate the net benefits of government projects consistent with your identified values?

Problems: Be sure to show your work.

1. You are offered the following information about a proposed government project: The costs of building the project will total $1100, with $600 of expense incurred immediately and $100 incurred over each of the five subsequent years. Benefits from the project will be $100 at the end of the second year, $200 at the end of the third year, and $300 per year from the end of the fourth year to the end of the eighth year.

   a) Assuming a social rate of discount of 10 percent, is this project viable?

b) How would your answer change if all of the expenses were incurred immediately?

c) Once again using the original information, at what discount rate will this project break even in the sense that discounted benefits will equal discounted costs? Note: This discount rate is known as the internal rate of return of the project.

2. Return to Problem 1 above and consider the new information that a sustained inflation of 5 percent per year is now projected. Assuming a nominal interest rate of 15 percent, what will be the net present value of this project? (Note: Assume that all the costs and benefits in the problem were calculated without any account of a possible inflation.)

SKETCH ANSWERS TO CHAPTER 6

Issue in Brief:

1. Automobiles, textiles, televisions, and pistachio nuts are among the industries that have been protected.

2. No, the distributional consequences of tariffs and quotas are significantly different. Tariffs capture the revenues from increased prices domestically, while quotas allow the "benefits" of the increased prices to flow out of the country and into the pockets of the foreign producers.

True/False:

1. F   It can not be easily evaluated.
2. T
3. T
4. F   They are different analytical techniques used for different types of decisions.
5. T
6. F   It compares programs of agencies with similar missions.
7. T
8. F   CB analysis is an old tool first used by the Army Corps of Engineers.
9. T
10. F   Both direct and indirect costs/benefits are considered.
11. T
12. T
13. T
14. F   The returns earned by investors are often different from those earned by savers.
15. T
16. F   The discount rate affects the ranking of alternative projects.
17. F   Inflation makes consistent measurement of costs and benefits a challenge.
18. F   Projects often get ranked differently by the two criteria.
19. T
20. F   This valuation is still very difficult and fraught with amibiguity.

Multiple Choice:

1.	e	6.	d	11.	d
2.	d	7.	a	12.	d
3.	c	8.	a	13.	b
4.	c	9.	b	14.	a
5.	b	10.	b	15.	c

Short Answer:

1. Compare your answer with those of your classmates. Try to be as honest as possible in evaluating your decision, because psychologically there is an incentive to reinforce the major decision you have already made. Cost-benefit analysis involves much effort. Do you feel that the benefits of this effort outweigh the costs for decisions such as the one you evaluated? The choice of an appropriate discount rate can be difficult, but some market rates on federal government securities can approximate a risk-free interest rate.

2. Compare your answer with those of your classmates. An obvious place where you might have (explicitly or implicitly) used cost-effectiveness analysis would be your choice of college or your choice of living arrangements at college.

3. For example, if you believe the poor have a special claim on societal resources or have needs that society should fulfill, their income share will receive disproportionately high weight in the cost-benefit analysis. Similarly, regions which you believe are deserving of special attention would be disproportionately weighted in the analysis.

Problems:

1.
   a) Yes, the project is viable. Discounted costs are $979.07 and discounted benefits are $1087.32.

   b) Discounted costs would now be $1100 and the project would no longer be viable.

   c) Through trying several discount rates in sequence, the internal rate of return can be quickly bracketed and then calculated with reasonable precision. The internal rate of return of this project is 12.9 percent.

2. Perhaps surprisingly, the answer here is the same as in part (a) of Problem 1. The costs and benefits are expressed in real terms in the problem and the real interest rate is (15 – 5) percent which is the 10 percent rate assumed in part (a). So, the net present value of the project is $108.25.

Chapter Recap: You should now be able to answer the following questions:

1. Explain the notion of program budgeting. Compare and contrast its merits with those of line-item budgeting.

2. What is cost-effectiveness analysis? How is it used in public sector decision-making?

3. What are the steps in cost-benefit analysis? How is such analysis used to determine the relative merits of government projects over time?

4. Discuss the difficulties in measuring the costs and benefits of public investment projects.

5. What is the social rate of discount? Explain its role in evaluating the present value of future benefits and costs.

6. Carefully discuss the role of cost-benefit analysis in the budgetary and political processes.

CHAPTER 7

Government Subsidies and Income Support for the Poor

Chapter Objectives: After reading and working through this chapter, you should understand:

1. The official definition of poverty in the United States and trends in poverty statistics.

2. The general demographic makeup of the poor in the United States.

3. The equity/efficiency tradeoffs in aiding the poor.

4. The collective benefits resulting from aid to the poor.

5. The concepts and applications of means and status tests for determining program eligibility.

6. The basic realm of major aid programs in the United States.

7. The nature of in-kind and cash transfers, as well as their relative importance and differing effects on individual choice.

8. The effects of transfer programs on resource allocation.

9. The effects of transfer programs on the work incentive of recipients.

10. The nature and relative merits of a negative income tax, wage rate subsidies, and the Earned Income Tax Credit as alternatives to our welfare system.

Chapter Summary:

1. This chapter examines the scope of major federal programs providing assistance to the poor in the United States. Poverty is defined and its magnitude discussed. Major federal programs are described and compared. A general framework is developed for analyzing the impact of subsidies and tranfers to individuals on the allocation of resources and on economic incentives.

2. Poverty in the United States is measured through comparison of a family's income with an established poverty threshold that is adjusted each year for changes in the cost of living. This threshold is based upon a multiple of the cost of a minimally acceptable diet and varies with family size and head of household characteristics. One problem with official poverty statistics is that they measure only cash income (including cash transfers) and do not include government transfers of goods and services to the poor.

3. A fundamental basis for income redistribution programs in the United States is as a system of "safety net" measures to prevent citizens' incomes from falling below minimally acceptable levels. There is great disagreement about what is minimally acceptable and thus much controversy about these programs. The problem is even more imperative since a substantial number of the poor are poor due to insufficient earnings rather than inability or unwillingness to work.

4. Income redistribution to the poor can be viewed as a public good. Nonpoor individuals can reap benefits from the insurance of a safety net to catch them should they hit hard times, from genuine compassion for their fellow humans, and from the increased social stability provided by a more equal distribution of income. The possibility of free riding associated with these collective benefits leads to public sector involvement in a realm simultaneously serviced by private charities.

5. Eligibility for programs is generally determined through use of a status and/or means test. The status test targets the individuals of certain groups for assistance (for example, displaced homemakers, Vietnam-era veterans). The means test establishes that applicants have assets and incomes below a minimally required amount in order to certify their eligibility for aid.

6. *Entitlement programs* are transfer programs that require payments to all those persons meeting eligibility requirements established by law.

7. Government programs to aid the poor consist of direct cash transfers, direct provision of basic goods and services, subsidies to assist the poor in obtaining basic goods and services, and employment and training programs designed to help the poor help themselves. The bulk of government aid is in the form of noncash assistance. Income support, social security, and welfare is the single largest category of spending in the federal budget.

8. Cash transfers tend to be a more efficient means of providing assistance to those in need, but cash transfer programs are unpalatable due to the lower level of accountability/control and high degree of fungibility of funds. In dollar terms, in-kind subsidies are much more important than cash transfers to the poor. In-kind subsidies are often justified by the fact that they allow some control over the spending patterns of recipients.

9. Assistance programs, especially in-kind ones, can distort the consumption, savings, work, and other behavior of individuals in ways that cause losses in efficiency. Subsidies that reduce prices to consumers below the market price are called *price-distorting subsidies* and are likely to result in losses in efficiency due to their substitution effects. Through altered choice patterns, such distortions reduce individual well-being below that achievable with an equivalent value cash subsidy.

10. *Fixed-allotment subsidies* give eligible recipients the right to consume a certain amount of a given good or service during a specified time period. Such subsidies may be given in the form of vouchers or as a direct allotment of the good or service. Such subsidies do not directly distort prices.

11. The new welfare program, Temporary Assistance to Needy Families (TANF), has changed the system of support to the poor in the United States. Expenditures under the program are now capped at the Federal level. Funds are allocated to states based on previous expenditures. Each states sets its own requirements for eligibility and most states now offer only limited assistance to people who do not agree to work. Lifetime eligibility per family is limited to five years of payments. The new system is designed to reduce the work disincentive effects of the income transfers.

12. A negative income tax has been suggested as an alternative to our welfare system. Such a program would be based upon cash assistance and integrated with the federal income tax. Unfortunately, with no status test, a program providing adequate benefits is likely to be prohibitively expensive.

13. A wage-rate subsidy program would take the place of the minimum wage. Government-subsidized wages would theoretically increase employment opportunities and provide incentives for workers to move to higher-paying jobs. The Earned Income Tax Credit is a variant of a wage-rate subsidy.

14. The Earned Income Tax Credit (EITC) has become a major means of income support for the working poor. It is only available to those who work and acts as a form of wage subsidy. The program provides a negative tax payment (not just a tax refund!) to low-income wage earners. Recent legislation has expanded eligibility for and raised the benefits available under the EITC.

15. Despite sharp increases in spending to aid the poor, the poor's income share has not substantially increased.

Issue in Brief: TANF—Tough New Standards for Income Support to the Poor

Temporary Assistance to Needy Families (TANF) now limits welfare payments to the poor in the United States. The Public Policy Perspective on pages 268-269 of the text discusses some of the key features of the new welfare system. The new system will limit payments to families to a maximum of 5 years and will require most able-bodied recipients to participate in activities that will help them become self-supporting. The new law also includes grants to subsidize child-care services to the poor and to reduce nonmaritial births. Recipients of income support under TANF with children over the age of 5 who refuse offers of work could lose their benefits. Actual administration of the program will vary by state.

Questions for Discussion:

1. Why is income under support for the poor under TANF no longer considered an entitlement program?

2. It remains to be seen whether or not the new program will survive an economic downturn. What could happen in a recession when job opportunities become scarce?

3. How could the new program decrease wages for unskilled workers?

4. How could the new program increase expenditure for the poor under the Earned Income Tax Credit (EITC) program?

CHAPTER REVIEW QUESTIONS

True/False Questions: If false, explain how to correct the statement to make it true.

1. Eligibility for most assistance programs varies from state to state.

2. In 1995 30 percent of the U.S. population was classified as poor.

3. Only about 11 percent of the elderly are classified as poor.

4. One problem with the official poverty statistics is that they measure only cash income.

5. There has been no fundamental revision in the system of U.S. support for the poor in nearly 30 years.

6. Very few poor families are poor because of insufficient earnings rather than inability to work.

7. Income redistribution to the poor can be viewed as a public good.

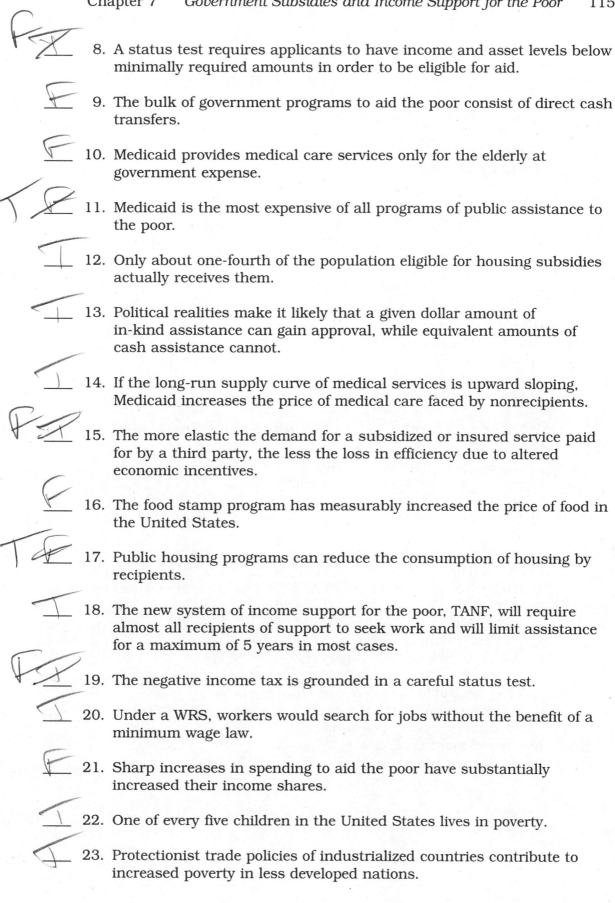

8. A status test requires applicants to have income and asset levels below minimally required amounts in order to be eligible for aid.

9. The bulk of government programs to aid the poor consist of direct cash transfers.

10. Medicaid provides medical care services only for the elderly at government expense.

11. Medicaid is the most expensive of all programs of public assistance to the poor.

12. Only about one-fourth of the population eligible for housing subsidies actually receives them.

13. Political realities make it likely that a given dollar amount of in-kind assistance can gain approval, while equivalent amounts of cash assistance cannot.

14. If the long-run supply curve of medical services is upward sloping, Medicaid increases the price of medical care faced by nonrecipients.

15. The more elastic the demand for a subsidized or insured service paid for by a third party, the less the loss in efficiency due to altered economic incentives.

16. The food stamp program has measurably increased the price of food in the United States.

17. Public housing programs can reduce the consumption of housing by recipients.

18. The new system of income support for the poor, TANF, will require almost all recipients of support to seek work and will limit assistance for a maximum of 5 years in most cases.

19. The negative income tax is grounded in a careful status test.

20. Under a WRS, workers would search for jobs without the benefit of a minimum wage law.

21. Sharp increases in spending to aid the poor have substantially increased their income shares.

22. One of every five children in the United States lives in poverty.

23. Protectionist trade policies of industrialized countries contribute to increased poverty in less developed nations.

Multiple Choice Questions: Choose the best answer.

1. Which of the following groups comprises the highest percentage of the poor?
   a) female heads of households.
   b) children.
   ~~c) male heads of households.~~
   d) elderly persons.

2. About what percent of dollars spent by governments in the United States is allocated to programs that support the poor?
   a) 5.
   b) 8.
   c) 10.
   d) 14.

3. The official poverty statistics:
   a) only count in-kind income.
   b) only count cash income.
   c) count both cash and in-kind income.
   d) understate the extent of poverty.

4. Which of the following notions does not provide justification for viewing income redistribution to the poor as a public good?
   a) the establishment of a safety net.
   b) genuine compassion for the unfortunate.
   c) the efficiency of in-kind transfers.
   d) increased social stability.

5. Assume that a particular welfare program is targeted at veterans, displaced homemakers, and children. Investigation of applicants to determine whether they are eligible for such a program would require a:
   a) status test.
   b) means test.
   c) physical examination.
   d) government audit.

6. Transfer programs in which those meeting both the means and the status test are automatically entitled to transfers are called:
   a) guaranteed income programs.
   b) basic support programs.
   c) entitlement programs.
   d) universal aid programs.

7. The largest cash transfer program for the poor is:
   a) TANF.
   b) Medicaid.
   c) SSI.
   d) Medicare.
   e) food stamps.

8. The most expensive of all programs to aid the poor is:
   a) TANF.
   b) Medicaid.
   c) SSI.
   d) Medicare.
   e) food stamps.

9. Which of the following programs has a means test?
   a) Social security pensions.   status
   b) unemployment insurance.   status
   c) veteran's benefits.   status
   d) food stamps.

10. Which of the following is not an in-kind benefit program?
    a) food stamps.
    b) SSI.
    c) energy assistance.
    d) Medicaid.

11. Medicaid does not provide aid for the:
    a) poor.
    b) blind.
    c) disabled.
    d) elderly.

12. Medicaid induces recipients to consume medical services up to the point where:
    a) MB = MC.
    b) MB > MC.
    c) TB = TC.
    d) MB = 0.

13. A cash subsidy designed to replace Medicaid and leave recipients just as well off would:
    a) cost more than the Medicaid program.
    b) cost less than the Medicaid program.
    c) increase distortions in the medical market.
    d) cost the same as Medicaid.

14. Under TANF which of the following is true?
    a) Federal support payments are made directly to all poor people who pass a means test.
    b) Federal payments to the states are capped based on expenditures in previous years so that TANF can no longer be considered a federal entilement program.
    c) Recipients of income support are not required to work.
    d) Poor people meeting a means test are eligible for income support for an indefinite period of time.

15. For most recipients of food stamps in the United States, if given an equivalent value cash subsidy, the recipient would:
    a) consume more food.
    b) consume less food.
    c) consume the same amount of food.
    d) consume a higher grade of food.

16. Substituting a cash subsidy for an equivalent price-distorting subsidy:
    a) will not affect the consumer's well being.
    b) will make the consumer better off.
    c) can not make the consumer worse off.
    d) will make the consumer worse off.

17. Which of the following distort a transfer recipient's choice of work or leisure?
    a) the means test.
    b) tax on earned income.
    c) reductions in benefits as earnings increase.
    d) all of the above.

18. Which of the following statements about a NIT is false?   Neg Inc Tax
    a) it would include in-kind assistance programs.
    b) it would provide a minimum income guarantee for all households.
    c) it would integrate government assistance with the federal income tax.
    d) the lower the phase-out rate of benefits, the more expensive will be the NIT.

19. Which of the following statements about wage-rate subsidies is false?
    a) under a WRS plan, minimum-wage legislation would be repealed.
    b) under a WRS plan, employers would generally be able to pay lower wages.
    c) under a WRS plan, employment opportunities would increase, but workers' incomes would decrease.
    d) the subsidy would vary with the wage paid and number of hours worked.

20. Since 1947, the percent share of aggregate money income (including cash transfers) going to the poor has:
    a) increased substantially.
    b) decreased substantially.
    c) remained about the same.
    d) increased, but only continually after 1967.

21. Which of the following represents a fixed allotment subsidy?
    a) Medicaid.
    b) food stamps.
    c) TANF.
    d) none of the above.

22. Single workers without children:
    a) can receive TANF.
    b) are ineligible for the EITC.
    c) are now eligible for the EITC.
    d) get the greatest amount of benefits under the EITC.

23. The EITC:
    a) is funded exclusively by the federal government.
    b) is only about five years old.
    c) has benefits that vary from state to state.
    d) now benefits about 5 million workers and families.

24. The EITC:
    a) is an in-kind subsidy program.
    b) provides assistance to disabled persons who cannot work.
    c) is more favorable to work effort than the negative income tax.
    d) none of the above.

Short Answer Questions: Answer in the space provided.

1. "Despite the sharp increases in spending to aid the poor, their income shares have not substantially increased." Based upon the information gained in this chapter, through outside reading, and through self-evaluation of your values, suggest a series of reforms in our government income support, welfare, and subsidy programs.

2. Carefully evaluate the costs and benefits associated with the use of status and means tests.

Problems: Be sure to show your work.

1. "Voluntary donations to the poor... are likely to result in an undersupply of income redistribution to low-income groups relative to the efficient amount." Using graphical analysis, show why this will be the case.

2. Can public housing increase the consumption of housing by recipients? Graphically illustrate such a case. Use the same notation as in Figure 7.5 in your textbook.

SKETCH ANSWERS TO CHAPTER 7

Issue in Brief:

1. Spending under an entitlement program is open-ended and will vary with vary with the number of eligible recipients. Under the new program expenditure each year are capped at the federal level and cannot increase even if the number of eligible recipients grows.

2. In a recession low-income recipients who have exhausted their welfare benefits would be destitute unless state and local governments provided additional funding for support or support could be funded through private charity. No additional federal support would be available during a recession unless Congress acts to provide it.

3. The supply of unskilled workers in labor markets will increase putting downward pressure on equilibrium wages.

4. The EITC pays benefits to the working poor. Because there will be more workers at low wage levels as a result of TANF, payments under the EITC will increase.

True/False:

1. T
2. F   Only about 14 percent of the polulation was classified as poor.
3. T
4. T
5. F   TANF, effective 1997, is a major revision of the system.
6. F   A substantial number are poor due to insufficient earnings.
7. T
8. F   This defines a means test.
9. F   Most are programs of direct provision of goods or services or subsidies.
10. F   It provides medical care for the poor under age 65.
11. T
12. T
13. T
14. T
15. F   The more elastic the demand, the greater the loss in efficiency.
16. F   The program has seemingly had little or no effect on the price of food.
17. T
18. T
19. F   There is no status test attached to the NIT.
20. T
21. F   Income shares have not changed much.
22. T
23. T

Multiple Choice:

1. b	6. c	11. d	16. c	21. b
2. d	7. a	12. d	17. d	22. c
3. b	8. b	13. b	18. a	23. a
4. c	9. d	14. b	19. c	24. c
5. a	10. b	15. c	20. c	

Short Answer:

1. Compare your answers with those of your classmates. Be sure to maintain consistency with your answers in Chapter 2.

2. Be sure to consider the transaction costs of the tests. Benefits include known direction of aid and reduced transaction costs through decision rules. Costs include the transaction costs of performing the test and the misdirection of aid which can occur by not considering individual circumstances.

Problems:

1.

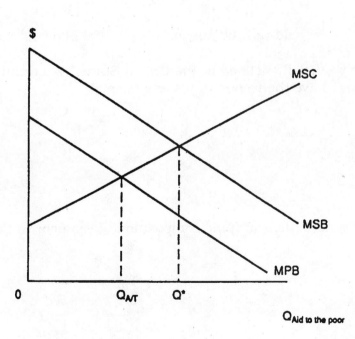

2. Expenditures on other goods

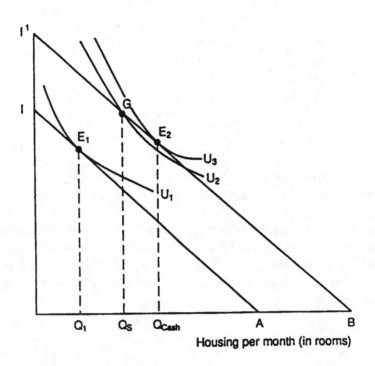

Housing per month (in rooms)

Chapter Recap: You should now be able to answer the following questions:

1. How is poverty officially defined in the United States? According to this definition, what have the trends in poverty been?

2. Describe the general demographic composition of the poor in the United States?

3. Describe the inherent efficiency/equity tradeoffs in aiding the poor.

4. What are the collective benefits resulting from aid to the poor?

5. What are means and status tests? How are they used to determine program eligibility?

6. Describe the realm the major programs to aid the poor in the United States.

7. Compare and contrast in-kind and cash-transfer programs. What is their relative importance in the United States?

8. Describe the effects of transfer programs on resource allocation.

9. What effect do transfer programs have on the work incentive of recipients?

10. Compare and contrast the negative income tax, wage-rate subsidies, and the Earned Income Tax Credit as alternatives to our present welfare system.

CHAPTER 8

Social Security and Social Insurance

Chapter Objectives: After reading and working through this chapter, you should understand:

1. The general nature of social insurance programs in the United States.

2. The differences between pay-as-you-go and fully funded pension systems.

3. The general provisions of the Social Security pension system in the United States.

4. The effects of Social Security pensions on disposable income, the distribution of income, and the incentives to work and save.

5. The challenge that changing demographics present to the Social Security pension system.

6. The general provisions of Medicare and its impact on the health-care market in the United States.

7. The general provisions of unemployment insurance and its impact on the labor market in the United States.

Chapter Summary:

1. This chapter focuses on the operation of social insurance programs administered under the Social Security Act in the United States. These programs include pensions, disability insurance, unemployment compensation, and health insurance for the elderly. Comparisons are made with other nations' social security systems.

2. Eligibility for benefits payable under Social Security programs in the United States is usually contingent upon paying a payroll tax or having such a tax paid on one's behalf by virtue of employment in a covered job. Social insurance and Social Security pensions do not have a means test per se, yet they are redistributive in nature.

3. *Social security* is a general term for a number of programs established by government to insure individuals against interruption or loss of earning power, as well as for expenditures resulting from marriage, maternity, children, sickness or injury, unemployment, or death. Such programs include government-provided pensions, disability payments, unemployment compensation, health benefits, and child-rearing assistance.

4. *A fully funded pension system* is one in which benefits are paid out of a fund built up from contributions by or on behalf of the recipients. The dollar value of the fund must be at least equal to the discounted present value of future pension liabilities. *A pay-as-you-go pension system* finances pensions for currently retired workers entirely by contributions or taxes paid by currently employed workers.

5. The bulk of payroll taxes collected to finance Social Security pensions in recent years have gone to financing the pensions of currently retired workers. Hence, Social Security has been effectively a pay-as-you-go system despite the existence of a Social Security trust fund. In an effort to compensate for the relatively larger proportion of retirees in the population in the early twenty-first century, payroll taxes and the retirement age have been recently raised and the trust fund has begun to grow. As today's relatively large cohort of workers retires in the twenty-first century, this trust fund will decline rapidly. In an effort to partially offset the effects of these demographic changes and higher life expectancies, legislation has been recently passed that will raise the retirement age to 67 by the year 2027.

6. The monthly pension that a worker receives upon retirement depends upon his/her earning history, years in covered employment, age at retirement, and family status. In addition, until age 70 an earnings test applies which limits the amount of earned income a worker can receive without reducing his/her pension.

7. Two measures used to evaluate the standard of living of Social Security pensioners as compared with their pre-pension days are the *gross replacement rate*, a ratio of the monthly retirement benefit to the monthly labor earnings in the year prior to retirement, and the *net replacement rate*, a ratio of the monthly retirement benefit to the worker's after-tax monthly labor earnings in the year prior to retirement. These replacement rates tend to be higher for lower income workers, as well as for workers with a dependent spouse. Net replacement rates tend to be higher than gross replacement rates. Most recently, these replacement rates have begun to decline due to legislative changes in the Social Security pension program and in the tax laws, but still remain well above the replacement rates that prevailed prior to 1970. Since 1972, Social Security pensions have been indexed to consumer prices.

8. Returns earned on Social Security taxes have declined as workers who have been employed their entire career under the system begin to retire, as payroll tax rates increase to keep the system solvent, and as the growth of the labor force subject to Social Security slows to a near halt as new sectors of coverage are exhausted and the birth rate slows down.

9. Three possible reforms have been suggested to prevent Social Security tax rates from increasing as much as scheduled in the 1990s: lower existing average replacement rates, change the structure of replacement rates, or increase the retirement age.

10. Although economic theory suggests that Social Security distorts both savings and work choices, there is no conclusive evidence confirming this, nor any that measures the actual effect. The impact of Social Security retirement benefits on economic incentives must account for the combined effect on the choices of both the recipients and financers of the benefits. Nevertheless, Social Security appears to discourage the elderly from working and most empirical studies find some evidence of a slight disincentive to save which can be attributed to Social Security.

11. Medicare provides health insurance for the elderly without respect to any means test. Medicare includes provisions for hospitalization insurance, catastrophic illness insurance, and for optional supplementary medical insurance. Medicare is faced with skyrocketing costs despite numerous cost-containment measures and faces many difficult policy decisions in the future.

12. Unemployment insurance is a state managed program whose revenue generation is administered by the federal government. Unemployment insurance is designed to provide temporary assistance for those out of work due to no fault of their own. There is some evidence that unemployment benefits act to increase the length of unemployment, but in many cases the benefits appear to allow workers to find higher wages and more stable employment.

Issue in Brief: Increasing the Retirement Age

As part of the last major amendments to the Social Security Act in 1983, the United States increased the minimum retirement age for full old-age social security benefits. The normal retirement age for full retirement benefits will be gradually increased beginning in the year 2003 from the present age 65 to a new minimum age of 67 in the year 2027. Thus, persons attaining age 62 in 2000 will be the first age cohort affected by the legislation.

The United States is but one of a large number of countries that have increased the minimum retirement age for full social security benefits. Interestingly, most of the legislation in other countries was pass after the U.S. amendments, but will be fully effective long before 2027. In addition, none of the other countries have raised their retirement age above 65, with several remaining at 60 years of age or below. Most countries have been motivated to raise their retirement age so as to reduce expenditures thereby improving government finance, but member nations of the European Union have also been trying to address the requirement that they equalize pension treatment of men and women (most countries had previously had a lower retirement age for women). In addition to the countries that have already raised their retirement ages, several Eastern European nations including Bulgaria and the Czech Republic have expressed the desire to do so. The possible unemployment effects of such an increase have acted as a deterrent thus far. For further information, see Joseph G. Simanis, "Worldwide Trend Toward Raising the Retirement Age," *Social Security Bulletin*, Summer 1994, pp. 83-84.

Questions for Discussion:

1. What is the primary reason for the slow phase-in of the new retirement age in the United States?

2. Without raising the retirement age or instituting a means test, how else could you reduce the rate of filing for retirement benefits?

CHAPTER REVIEW QUESTIONS

True/False Questions: If false, explain how to correct the statement to make it true.

_____ 1. The United States, in comparison with major European countries, was relatively tardy in passing social insurance legislation.

_____ 2. It is generally only the major industrialized countries that have some form of social security system.

_____ 3. Over the past 20 years, the average real income of the elderly in the United States increased faster than the average real income of the rest of the population.

_____ 4. Eligibility for benefits payable under the Social Security system is determined by a means test.

_____ 5. Self-employed individuals are not covered by the Social Security system.

_____ 6. FICA taxes consist of both employee and employer payroll taxes.

_____ 7. Unemployment insurance taxes are levied on both employers and employees.

____ 8. The way in which benefits are paid under Social Security programs results in income redistribution.

____ 9. The OASDI pension system is an example of a fully funded pension system.

____ 10. As the twenty-first century nears, the Social Security trust fund has begun to build up.

____ 11. The balance in the Social Security trust fund is equal to the discounted present value of all future pension benefits.

____ 12. A worker's insurance amount under Social Security is calculated independently of personal circumstances.

____ 13. Workers over age 70 are not subject to an earnings test with respect to their Social Security benefits.

____ 14. Only those who have worked in a covered job can receive a Social Security pension.

____ 15. Two workers with identical earnings histories may receive Social Security pensions of different amounts.

____ 16. The gross replacement rate declines as monthly earnings rise for workers.

____ 17. Gross replacement rates cannot exceed 100 percent.

____ 18. The gross replacement rate overestimates the extent to which Social Security benefits replace a retiree's disposable earnings.

____ 19. The method of indexing retirement benefits under Social Security is often criticized for being overgenerous.

____ 20. Social Security payroll tax rates have increased sharply since 1970.

____ 21. The proportion of retirees relative to the working population has been, and will continue, decreasing.

____ 22. The social security system reduces one's incentive to work after age 65.

____ 23. The induced-retirement effect suggests that Social Security may increase workers' incentive to save.

____ 24. Hospital benefits under Medicare are not subject to a deductible.

____ 25. Benefits under Medicare are "means tested."

_____ 26. Medicare distorts the consumption of medical services in much the same way as Medicaid.

_____ 27. Unemployment insurance policies are widely available from private insurance firms.

_____ 28. Currently, unemployment insurance benefits are fully taxable as personal income under the federal income tax.

Multiple Choice Questions: Choose the best answer.

_____ 1. The first social security legislation was enacted by which country?
a) Germany.
b) United States.
c) Soviet Union.
d) Sweden.
e) France.

_____ 2. Social Security administered programs include:
a) disability payments.
b) health benefits.
c) pensions.
d) survivors' benefits.
e) all of the above.

_____ 3. To be eligible for benefits under Social Security, a worker:
a) must not be covered by any other pension program.
b) must have dependents.
c) can not be self-employed.
d) generally must have 40 quarters of coverage.
e) must pass a means test.

_____ 4. A pension system that finances pensions for currently retired workers entirely by contributions or taxes paid by currently employed workers is:
a) fiscally unsound.
b) a pay-as-you-go system.
c) a fully funded system.
d) a tax-financed pension system.
e) dependent upon asymmetric information.

_____ 5. Average indexed monthly earnings (AIME):
a) do not account for changes in the general price level.
b) consider all labor earnings by the worker.
c) take into consideration a worker's age of retirement.
d) all of the above.

____ 6. The Social Security earnings test:
   a) applies only to workers between 65 and 69 years of age.
   b) reduces Social Security benefits for all employed workers subject to it.
   c) carries an implicit tax rate of 50 percent.
   d) all of the above.

____ 7. Which of the following workers will have the lowest gross replacement rate?
   a) a single high-income worker.
   b) a married high-income worker with a dependent spouse.
   c) a single low-income worker.
   d) a married low-income worker with a dependent spouse.

____ 8. Two earner households receive Social Security pension benefits:
   a) equal to twice the benefits of the spouse with higher earnings.
   b) equal to twice the benefits of the spouse with lower earnings.
   c) no less than 1.5 times the benefit of the spouse with higher earnings.
   d) equal to the sum of the benefits earned by each spouse due to their employment.

____ 9. Which of the following statements is true?
   a) GRR < NRR.
   b) GRR = NRR.
   c) GRR > NRR.
   d) none of the above.

____ 10. Social Security pension benefits:
   a) are taxable for all retirees.
   b) are nontaxable for all retirees.
   c) are subject to state but not federal income taxes.
   d) are subject to income taxes when the recipient's income exceeds a certain amount.

____ 11. Which of the following accounted for the largest percent of the income of the aged in 1986?
   a) private and government employee pensions.
   b) Social Security pensions.
   c) income from past saving.
   d) labor income.

____ 12. Adjusting for inflation, the rate of growth of wages per worker in the United States has averaged about what percent per year since the Social Security system has been in operation?
   a) 6.
   b) 1.
   c) 2.
   d) 4.

____ 13. Which of the following contributed to higher average returns on Social Security taxes paid for workers retiring in the 1970's?
a) increased labor force participation rates.
b) increased tax rates.
c) coverage of new industries and jobs by the system.
d) coverage of the self-employed by the system.
e) all of the above.

____ 14. The Social Security system transfers income from:
a) retirees to workers.
b) single workers to married workers with dependent spouses.
c) married workers with dependent spouses to two-earner couples.
d) low-income workers to high-income workers.

____ 15. Which of the following is not expected to happen by the early part of the twenty-first century?
a) an increase in the proportion of retirees relative to the working population.
b) an increase in the retirement age.
c) an increase in the maximum earnings subject to payroll taxes.
d) a decrease in replacement rates.
e) none of the above.

____ 16. About what proportion of unemployed American workers actually collect unemployment insurance benefits?
a) 10 percent.
b) 25 percent.
c) 33 percent.
d) 50 percent.
e) 75 percent.

____ 17. Empirical evidence on the savings and work incentive distortions of Social Security indicate:
a) no clear conclusions.
b) Social Security decreases the work incentive and increases savings.
c) Social Security decreases savings, but its effect on the work incentive is inconclusive.
d) Social Security decreases the work incentive, but its effect on savings is inconclusive.

____ 18. Participation of the elderly in the labor force has:
a) declined steadily since 1940.
b) increased steadily since 1940.
c) remained about the same since 1940.
d) fluctuated greatly since 1940 with no clear trend.

____ 19. Which of the following reduces the incentive to save?
   a) the induced-retirement effect.
   b) the bequest effect.
   c) the asset-substitution effect.
   d) diminishing marginal utility of capital.

____ 20. Supplementary medical insurance for doctor's services is provided under:
   a) Medicare Part A.
   b) Medicare Part B.
   c) AFDC.
   d) Medicaid.

____ 21. The process by which persons who have the greatest probability of obtaining benefits seek to obtain insurance and conceal their poor risk status is called:
   a) risk-sharing.
   b) adverse selection.
   c) moral hazard.
   d) fraud of the third degree.

____ 22. Unemployment insurance:
   a) is an automatic stabilizer in the federal budget.
   b) is available to all of the 97 percent of workers covered by the unemployment insurance system.
   c) benefits are normally limited to 26 weeks.
   d) benefits are currently fully taxable as personal income.
   e) all of the above.

Short Answer Questions: Answer in the space provided.

1. In the face of sharply rising costs and the projected HI trust fund shortfall, Medicare is in crisis. Suggest some aggressive reforms designed to head-off the crisis. Assess the political palatability of your suggested reforms. (Return to this question after completing Chapter 9 and reevaluate your answer based on the additional learning you have done.)

2. Evaluate the redistributive nature of Social Security in terms of the values you set out in your answers to the short-answer questions in Chapter 2 in this study guide. Note any reform suggestions that you would make.

Problems: Be sure to show your work.

1. Do Problem 3 in your textbook. Now assume that the Social Security benefit reduction rate is increased to a $1 reduction for each $2 of labor earnings. How does your answer to Problem 3 change? To what degree is your answer dependent upon the shape of the indifference curves? What are the policy implications of such an increase in the benefit reduction rate?

2. "For some retired workers, a dollar of earnings will result in both taxes and loss of Social Security benefits that will exceed the dollar of earnings!" Illustrate this graphically using a model like that in Figure 8.2.

SKETCH ANSWERS TO CHAPTER 8

Issue in Brief:

1. The phase-in will allow people to adjust their savings and retirement planning behavior to account for the age change. Those persons who will be the first fully affected by the age 67 rule were 23 years of age at the time of the passage of the legislation.

2. Some countries have increased the minimum insurance period for pension eligibility (i.e., how many years one must work before being eligible for pension coverage). One could also place a maximum on the number of years of pension one could collect, although this would not necessarily be politically feasible or desirable.

True/False:

1. T
2. F   More than 140 countries have some form of social security system.
3. T
4. F   There is no means test for Social Security.
5. F   They are covered.
6. T
7. F   It is only levied on employers.
8. T
9. F   The system is not fully funded.

10. T
11. F   The balance runs on average at about only one year's worth of benefits.
12. F   It does take account of personal circumstances.
13. T
14. F   For example, dependent nonworking spouses or widows receive benefits.
15. T
16. T
17. F   They can exceed 100 percent.
18. F   It underestimates the replacement.
19. T
20. T
21. F   It has been, and will continue, increasing.
22. T
23. T
24. F   There is a deductible.
25. F   The benefits are not means tested.
26. T
27. F   They are not generally available in the private market.
28. T

Multiple Choice:

1. a	6. a	11. b	16. c	21. b
2. e	7. a	12. c	17. a	22. e
3. d	8. c	13. e	18. a	
4. b	9. a	14. b	19. c	
5. c	10. d	15. e	20. b	

Short Answer:

1. Compare your answers with those of your classmates. What are the prospects for any of your reforms taking place? What are the barriers that must be surmounted?

2. Your textbook notes several of the redistributions that Social Security performs. Here again, evaluation of such a redistribution involves normative economics and as such a consideration of one's underlying values. A comparison with the answers of your classmates may be enlightening.

Problems:

1. The worker will reduce the amount he/she works. There is a reduced work incentive due to the increased benefit reduction rate. The greater the preference for leisure (as reflected in the shape of the indifference curves), the greater the reduction in work hours.

2. The region of the budget line in which the prohibitive tax/benefit reduction rate combination applies will be upward sloping (unlike the downward sloping region FH in Figure 8.2). In such a circumstance, convex indifference curves will lead the worker not to work any hours for which the prohibitive confiscation formula would apply.

Chapter Recap: You should now be able to answer the following questions:

1. Describe the general nature of social insurance programs in the United States.

2. Contrast pay-as-you-go and fully funded pension systems.

3. What are the general provisions of the Social Security pension system in the United States?

4. What effects does Social Security have on the distribution of income and the incentives to work and save?

5. What special challenges face Social Security as population demographics change in the late twentieth century?

6. Outline the Medicare program in the United States. What effects does the program have on the health-care market?

7. Describe the unemployment insurance system in the United States. How does the system affect the market for labor?

CHAPTER 9

Government and Health Care

Chapter Objectives: After reading and working through this chapter, you should understand:

1. The general structure of health-care expenditures in the United States.

2. Government's role in health-care finance in the United States.

3. The nature of third-party payments for health-care services and the effect of such payments on economic incentives and the market for those services.

4. The unique features of the market for health care and the reasons for the high rates of increase in the prices for medical services in the United States in recent years.

5. The basic benefits structure of the Medicare and Medicaid programs in the United States.

6. Alternative means that might be used to control the growth of spending on health care.

7. Alternatives for direct government provision of medical services or national health insurance in the United States, including universal entitlement programs.

Chapter Summary:

1. This chapter focuses on discussion of economic issues relating to health care and health insurance, including the role of government in the health-care market. The means by which a system of third-party payments for medical services affects incentives to consume and supply such services is explored. Mechanisms and policy alternatives for more efficiently allocating resources to health care, stemming the rise in health-care expenditures, as well as financing and rationing medical and health-care services are investigated.

2. Expenditures on health care in the United States have been rising rapidly. The share of GDP allocated to health care has nearly tripled since 1960 and amounted to 13.5 percent of GDP in 1995. More than 46 percent of U.S. health-care expenditures in 1995 were financed by governments, while only about one-fifth were financed out-of-pocket by individuals. These individual out-of-pocket expenses have been dropping in relative terms since 1965.

3. The bulk of government expenditures for health care are made through direct payments to physicians, hospitals, and other health care providers through Medicare and Medicaid. Governments also pay medical expenses for disabled workers through workers' compensation programs, for military personnel through defense department operations, and for veterans through various targeted assistance programs. State and local governments often operate and/or subsidize public hospitals.

4. A large amount of health-care spending is financed by indirect government subsidies to private health insurance. These subsidies include preferential tax treatment of employee and employer contributions for private health insurance. The Congressional Budget Office has estimated that the exclusion of employer paid health insurance benefits from the taxable incomes of employees cost the federal government alone over $75 billion in revenue in 1998. Such tax preferences also distort the employee's choice between cash and noncash compensation, further imposing an economic cost.

5. The system of health insurance in the United States has increasingly moved toward coverage of all medical expenses, subject to maximum benefits and deductibles as well as coinsurance clauses, rather than merely covering low-probability medical expenses. This has reduced price consciousness among health-care consumers, as well as impaired the ability of the market system to ration health-care services. High insurance premiums and increased use of "experience rating" are but two consequences of the operation of our present health-care insurance system.

6. The system of health-care provision in the United States is substantially one of *third-party payments*, where the third party is neither the purchaser nor the seller of the service. Most insurance plans include provisions for a *deductible*, a requirement that patients incur an initial level of expenditures before the plan starts paying benefits, and *coinsurance*, provisions that require patients to share in the payment of covered health-care costs above the level of the deductible (typically up to some maximum out-of-pocket contribution or maximum total plan benefit in a particular year). Both the deductible and coinsurance increase cost awareness, but the system of third-party payments increases the incentive to both consume and provide health-care services, inefficiently increasing the amount of resources devoted to health care and the quantity of health-care services provided in the marketplace.

7. The *moral hazard of health insurance* is the increase in the incentives to consume and supply health-care services that results from the reduction in price to consumers when third parties pay the bulk of medical expenses. Consumers agree to more procedures and prescriptions than they might in the absence of insurance. In addition, coverage by insurance reduces the incentive to take adequate precautions against incurring an insured expense. The magnitude of moral hazard depends on the elasticity of demand for health-care services.

8. Physicians dominate decisionmaking in the market for health care. They prescribe medications and procedures, controlling access to medical technology. Patients find access to information about alternative treatments and providers difficult to obtain, and market competition and market entry are severely limited by rules and tradition. The ability of physicians to generate demand for medical services is an important consideration in designing policies to control health-care expenditures.

9. High malpractice insurance costs, the "cross-subsidization" of patients who are unable to afford to pay for medical care or insurance on their own, and rapid technological change coupled with the desire on the part of both physicians and patients to use the most advanced tools and techniques of modern medicine also have contributed to increased health care and health insurance costs.

10. The bulk of the United States population is covered under our health insurance system, but significant gaps in coverage still exist. Currently, about 15 percent of the United States population under the age of 65 have no health insurance, up from 12.5 percent in 1980. As jobs shift to the service sector, fewer workers are covered by employer insurance plans. Part-time workers are also generally not eligible for, or covered by, employer-provided health insurance. Initial waiting periods can also leave short term and mobile workers uncovered for long periods of time. People not in the labor force represent about one-fifth of those without health insurance coverage. Such persons often find the costs and requirements of individual health insurance policies to be prohibitive.

11. Although Medicaid pays virtually all of the health-care costs of its beneficiaries, Medicare pays only 45 percent of the total health costs of the aged and disabled who are eligible for coverage. This is in part due to the lack of a Medicare out-of-pocket cost cap. Most Medicare recipients thus also rely on supplementary health insurance from their former employer or a "medigap" policy purchased from a private insurer. Recall that indigent Medicare patients are also eligible for benefits under the Medicaid program.

12. Various reforms have been suggested to help control spending on health care and to improve the efficiency in the mix of services provided by the U.S. health-care system. Increasing the out-of-pocket price of health-care services to the individuals that use them can be accomplished by higher deductibles

and coinsurance rates for consumers. These provisions would help reduce the incentive to overconsume medical services that exists in the present health-care system.

13. An alternative means to help control the overallocation of resources to health-care services would be to directly intervene in the decisions of health-care providers and patients through a system of managed care. A managed-care system would require the decisions of health-care prescribers to be reviewed for appropriateness and would require patients to purchase health-care services from a specified network of health-care providers. The insurance firms sponsoring such managed-care systems typically provide incentives to economize on the use of medical resources by using some variant of *capitation payments* (payments that vary with the number of patients served rather than the number of services provided). Health Maintenance and Preferred Provider Organizations are variants of managed-care systems.

14. The most direct and drastic ways of government intervention in the market for health-care services to control expenditures are direct controls on prices and regulation of the volume of services supplied. Medicare and Medicaid have experimented with such price controls and with review procedures. They have had a mixed experience with such efforts, both in terms of success and in terms of acceptance.

15. Direct government provision of medical services is an additional reform option. To the extent that health-care services have public good attributes, such intervention can be justified in a straight-forward fashion, as can intervention to improve information flow in the market and regulation to assure quality health care. On the other hand, the equity and income inequality aspects of health-care provision programs are far more controversial and require significant normative evaluation. As might be expected, a variety of proposals ranging from catastrophic coverage for the indigent to comprehensive health coverage for all citizens have been put forth with various means for implementation. Unfortunately, a national health insurance program would still require some non-market means of rationing health care, a very difficult issue to deal with.

16. A universal entitlement system could build upon our present health care insurance system by mandating that all employers provide insurance. The government would fill the remaining gaps through new programs and subsidies to aid the unemployed, those out of the labor force, or those who are still not covered by health insurance.

Issue in Brief: Long Term Care

One of *Governing* magazine's 1994 Innovations in State and Local Government Awards went to an innovative program of the New York State Department of Social Services. Faced with the familiar issue of middle-class residents who needed nursing home care being forced to spend down their savings or transfer assets out of their estates so as to establish eligibility for Medicaid, the state formed a partnership with the state's insurance companies that protects the state, consumers, and the insurance companies against catastrophic losses. Consumers and the state receive their protection at the front end, with an insurance policy paying for up to three years of nursing home care or six years of in home care. Consumers and insurance companies are protected at the back end. At the end of three years (which is also the average length of stay at a nursing home), the state's Medicaid program steps in and pays for care as long as it is needed. For participants who buy a policy with the Partnership for Long-Term Care, the state eliminates the asset test for Medicaid eligibility (income must still be used to defray costs before Medicaid kicks in). For further information, see Penelope Lemov, "Long-Term Care Without Poverty," *Governing*, October 1994, p. 44.

Questions for Discussion:

1. Why was the State of New York motivated to form such a partnership with the insurance companies?

2. What do you suppose happened to the sales of long-term care insurance policies in New York?

CHAPTER REVIEW QUESTIONS

True/False Questions: If false, explain how to correct the statement to make it true.

_____ 1. In the United States, we spend much more per person for health care than do citizens of other nations.

_____ 2. During the 1980s and 1990s, prices for medical services rose at about the same rate as prices for other goods and services on average.

_____ 3. The share of GDP allocated to health care in the United States has nearly tripled since 1960.

_____ 4. The portion of health-care expenses paid by Americans out of pocket has been declining since 1965.

_____ 5. The Medicare program accounts for the largest amount of government direct spending on health care in the United States.

____   6. Medicare benefits are subject to strict limits that are less generous than most private health insurance programs.

____   7. Medicare and Medicaid are administered by state governments.

____   8. Under the present United States tax system, health insurance is worth more to employees than an equivalent number of dollars of cash income.

____   9. The United States health insurance system primarily insures low-probability medical expenses.

____   10. The system of third-party payments increases the incentive to both consume and provide health-care services.

____   11. Medicaid programs administered by the states place few limits on reimbursement rates.

____   12. There has been a tremendous increase in the supply of physicians since 1970 in the United States.

____   13. Physicians have the ability to generate demand for medical services.

____   14. Uninsured and insured patients are often charged different prices for health-care services.

____   15. As of 1992, it was estimated that about ten million people in the United States under the age of 65 had no health insurance.

____   16. The proportion of the uninsured in the United States has fallen since 1980.

____   17. Medicare places no annual limit on out-of-pocket costs by beneficiaries.

____   18. Most employer-based health insurance plans provide benefits for long-term care services.

____   19. The structure of the health insurance system in the United States results in high administrative costs.

____   20. The Prospective Payment System used by Medicare gives hospitals a fixed payment per patient for the expected costs of treating patients with specific illnesses.

____   21. The average reimbursement rate to hospitals under Medicaid is well below hospital costs of services.

____ 22. The federal government has imposed requirements that employers offering health insurance offer an HMO option to their enrollees.

____ 23. Under the current health-care system in the United States, ability to pay is chiefly determined by income.

____ 24. A national health insurance system would still have to face issues of rationing health-care services.

____ 25. One of every three dollars spent under Medicaid pays for health care for the elderly.

____ 26. A universal entitlement system could reduce the total health insurance premiums employers pay.

____ 27. Persons currently on Medicaid would have a reduced work incentive if we moved to a universal entitlement system.

Multiple Choice Questions: Choose the best answer.

____ 1. Recent projections by the Congressional Budget Office indicate that health-care spending will account for what share of the federal budget by 2000?
a) 10 percent.
b) 20 percent.
c) 25 percent.
d) 33 percent.

____ 2. Private and government insurance programs pays about what percent of medical bills for UNITED STATES citizens?
a) 15.
b) 25.
c) 40.
d) 60.
e) 80.

____ 3. What level of government accounts for the largest share of health care spending?
a) federal.
b) state.
c) municipal.
d) special district.

____   4. Which of the following programs accounts for the largest portion of public health expenditure in the United States?
    a) veteran's hospitals.
    b) medical research.
    c) Medicare.
    d) Medicaid.
    e) workers compensation.

____   5. Medicare:
    a) is a government entitlement program.
    b) provides hospital insurance to all eligible persons.
    c) requires those desiring its supplementary medical insurance to pay a modest monthly fee.
    d) benefits are subject to strict limits that are less generous than most private health insurance programs.
    e) all of the above.

____   6. Medicaid:
    a) is administered by the federal government.
    b) limits personal spending on health care by individuals.
    c) is only available to welfare recipients.
    d) all of the above.
    e) none of the above.

____   7. Favorable tax treatment of employer and employee contributions for health care and health insurance benefits includes:
    a) exemption from taxable income of employer contributions for health insurance.
    b) special plans that allow employees to exclude their contributions for health insurance and qualified health care expenses from taxable income.
    c) an itemized deduction for large health care expenditures.
    d) all of the above.

____   8. After a certain minimum cost incurred by the patient, an insurance plan pays 80 percent of covered expenses. The 20 percent paid by the patient is referred to as:
    a) a deductible.
    b) coinsurance.
    c) cross-subsidization.
    d) an in-kind expenditure.

____   9. Which of the following is *not* a consequence of third-party payments?
    a) reduced out-of-pocket prices of services for patients.
    b) increased prices received by health-care providers.
    c) reduced resources devoted to health care.
    d) prescription of a larger number of tests and health-care services than would be otherwise prescribed.

____ 10. "Coverage by insurance reduces the incentive to take adequate precautions against incurring an insured expense." This quote refers to what concept?
   a) moral hazard.
   b) risk aversion.
   c) insurance fraud.
   d) rational self-interest.

____ 11. The increased supply of physicians in the United States has:
   a) put downward pressure on the price of some medical services.
   b) decreased incomes for physicians.
   c) led to physicians' attempts to increase demand for the services they generate.
   d) all of the above.
   e) a and c only.

____ 12. Which of the following is *not* a factor that has influenced the rising cost of medical services?
   a) the ability of physicians to generate demand for medical services.
   b) malpractice insurance rates.
   c) "cross-subsidization" of patients.
   d) community rating of risks.
   e) none of the above.

____ 13. About what portion of the uninsured under the age of 65 have jobs?
   a) 10 percent.
   b) 20 percent.
   c) 40 percent.
   d) 50 percent.
   e) 75 percent.

____ 14. Medicare pays about what percent of the total health costs of its eligible recipients?
   a) 45.
   b) 60.
   c) 80.
   d) 90.

____ 15. Capitation payments:
   a) encourage physicians to prescribe large amounts of tests and other health-care services.
   b) are typically incurred by patients.
   c) vary with the number of patients served.
   d) all of the above.

____ 16. A national health insurance system in the United States:
   a) would solve our present problems of rationing health care.
   b) would require the government to be the sole health insurer.
   c) will not necessarily stem the rate of growth of medical expenses.
   d) all of the above.

____ 17. Under the British Health Service:
   a) there is no private provision of hospital services.
   b) budgeting for capital expenditures is done by the government.
   c) emergency care is difficult to obtain.
   d) few people are on waiting lists for surgery.

Short Answer Questions: Answer in the space provided.

1. Are you or your family covered by health insurance? (If you and your family are not covered, try to answer the following series of questions on the basis of information from a health insurance brochure or advertisement.) What is the policy deductible? Are there coinsurance provisions? Are routine medical services covered? What are the hospitalization benefits under the plan? Are there annual maximums for out-of-pocket costs?

2. Investigate the availability of HMOs in your area. How do the premiums and service prices for HMOs in your area compare to more traditional health insurance plans and fee-for-service physician prices?

Problem: Be sure to show your work.

1. Using the graph from Problem 2 in your textbook, show how an increased deductible can reduce the loss in efficiency that results from third-party payments.

2. Show that the more elastic the demand for health-care services, the greater the magnitude of moral hazard.

SKETCH ANSWERS TO CHAPTER 9

Issue in Brief:

1. The high cost of long-term care was being borne by the state, partially due to the incentives present in the status quo.

2. Sales of policies more than doubled since the program's inception, as compared with flat sales in other states without such a program.

True/False:

1. T
2. F   Medical services prices rose twice as fast.
3. T
4. T
5. T
6. T
7. F   Medicare is administered by the federal government.
8. T
9. F   High probability expenses are widely insured.
10. T
11. F   Stringent limits are placed on reimbursement rates.
12. T

13. T
14. T
15. F   About 35 million people had no health insurance.
16. F   The proportion has grown.
17. T
18. F   Long-term care is generally not covered.
19. T
20. T
21. T
22. T
23. F   It is chiefly determined by health insurance coverage.
24. T
25. T
26. T
27. F   Work incentive would likely increase.

Multiple Choice:

1. c	6. e	11. e	16. c
2. e	7. d	12. d	17. b
3. a	8. b	13. d	
4. c	9. c	14. a	
5. e	10. a	15. c	

Short Answer:

1. Compare your answers with those of your classmates. How much variance in plans do you observe? Is any plan clearly superior or inferior to the others?

2. Compare your answer with those of your classmates. HMOs vary in their availability by area of the country and enroll a varying proportion of the local population based on their reputation and degree of establishment (as well as the service they provide and their premiums).

Problems:

1. Consumers who do not exceed the deductible level in medical-care costs will pay the full price of the services they consume. In much the same way as the Medicaid market was segmented in our Chapter 7 analysis, the higher the deductible, the fewer consumers who will exceed the deductible, and the less will be the total overconsumption of health care (thus the lower the loss in net benefits from overallocation of resources, *ceteris paribus*).

2. Experiment with the diagram accompanying Problem 2 in your textbook.

Chapter Recap: You should now be able to answer the following questions:

1. Describe the general structure of health-care expenditures in the United States.

2. Describe government's role in health-care finance in the United States.

3. What are third-party payments for health-care services? What are the economic effects of a system of such payments?

4. Describe the unique features of the market for health care.

5. Carefully discuss the reasons for the high rates of increase in the prices for medical services in the United States.

6. Discuss alternative means that might be used to control the growth of spending on health care.

7. Describe the basic benefit structure of Medicare and Medicaid in the United States.

8. Describe alternatives for direct government provision of medical services or national health insurance in the United States, including universal entitlement systems.

CHAPTER 10

Introduction to Government Finance

Chapter Objectives: After reading and working through this chapter, you should understand:

1. The effects of means of finance on important economic and political variables.

2. The benefit and ability-to-pay principles of government finance.

3. The notions of horizontal and vertical equity.

4. The basic principles of taxation and tax structure.

5. The criteria for evaluating alternative methods of government finance.

6. The distinction between tax evasion and tax avoidance.

7. The nature and use of nontax means of government finance.

8. The pricing of congestible government-supplied services and the products of government enterprises.

Chapter Summary:

1. This chapter begins an exploration of government finance. The economic basis of government finance is discussed, as well as criteria for evaluating alternative methods of government finance. Basic principles of taxation are explained, and nontax methods of government finance are introduced and considered.

2. Government activity requires the reallocation of resources from private to government use. Government finance tools act to perform this reallocation. The means of finance differ in their methods of operation and their effects on the political equilibrium, market equilibrium, efficiency, and the distribution of income in the economy.

3. The absence of a direct link between the benefits of government-provided goods and services and their finance creates unique problems in choosing a method of revenue generation. The collective benefits associated with these same goods and services further complicate attempts to allocate costs among individuals. Similarly, congestion makes allocation difficult. In general, governments' attempt to distribute the burden of finance among citizens is based upon either the *benefit principle*, which argues that the financing means should be linked to the benefits that individual citizens receive from government, or the *ability-to-pay principle*, which argues that the financing means should be linked to the capacity of individual citizens to contribute to the finance of government.

4. *Horizontal equity* is achieved when individuals with the same economic capacity bear the same burden of financing government activity. *Vertical equity* is achieved when individuals with differing economic capacity bear burdens of government finance which differ based upon some collectively chosen notion of fairness. These two concepts can be used to judge financing mechanisms which are founded on the ability-to-pay principle. Unfortunately, application of these concepts proves to be very complex due to the great difficulty in tracing out the effects of a finance tool on the distribution of income, not to mention the subjectivity of the criteria.

5. *Taxes* are the most commonly used form of government finance. They represent compulsory payments associated with certain activities. The item or activity on which the tax is levied is called the *tax base*, while the size of the tax relative to the base is called the *tax rate*. The *tax rate structure* expresses the relationship between the tax collected over a given accounting period and the tax base. Tax rate structures include proportional, progressive, and regressive tax rate structures. Under a proportional tax rate structure, the average tax rate is constant. Under a progressive tax structure, the average tax rate increases with the size of the tax base. Finally, under a regressive tax structure, the average tax rate declines with increases in the tax base.

6. Criteria for evaluating alternative methods of government finance include efficiency, equity, and administrative ease. These criteria are very likely to conflict and tend to be difficult to evaluate.

7. Alternative financing tools to taxation include: direct appropriation, debt finance, government-induced inflation, donations, user charges and earmarked taxes, and government enterprise. User charges, earmarked taxes, and government enterprise attempt to directly implement the benefit principle.

Issue in Brief: Lottery Mania

The popularity of state lotteries (as well as other forms of legalized gambling) has mushroomed since the mid 1980s. In 1980 only fourteen states had a lottery, while by the end of 1993 thirty-seven states and the District of Columbia operated lotteries. Despite their popularity, lotteries have proven to be an inefficient means of raising revenues due to their high administrative costs and the difficulty in sustaining play after the novelty wears off and when alternative forms of gambling increasingly compete for players' dollars. On average, states keep less than half (typically closer to forty percent) of lottery proceeds as revenues. Typically, modest state sales tax increases (one percentage point or less) would generate a similar revenue stream. But lotteries also remain popular because most states designate lottery revenues for a specific program or programs. The most popular use of lottery funds is for education, but the fungibility of revenues has typically meant that *total* spending has not increased on those programs designated to receive lottery revenues. Increasingly, lottery funds have been an unstable source of revenues despite increased promotional efforts and rules changes designed to increase the size of jackpots (by paradoxically decreasing the chances of winning any single game). For further information, see John Brittain, "Behind Lottery Mania: What Southeastern States Can Expect," *Regional Update*, Federal Reserve Bank of Atlanta, Volume 6, Numbers 2-3, 1993, pp. 6-8.

Questions for Discussion:

1. Does your state have a lottery? What different games are available? How often are new games introduced?

2. What are some of the competitors for lottery dollars?

3. What federal legislation substantially increased the presence of casino gambling in the United States?

CHAPTER REVIEW QUESTIONS

True/False Questions: If false, explain how to correct the statement to make it true.

F 1. Taxes account for about 60 percent of total government revenue. (higher)

T 2. The choice of government finance tool can affect the overall market equilibrium.

T 3. Those who subscribe to the benefit principle advocate fees and charges as ideal forms of government finance.

___ 4. If all citizens are taxed according to their ability to pay, Lindahl Equilibrium would result, provided the free-rider problem did not exist.

___ 5. Application of the ability-to-pay principle requires a collective agreement concerning a notion of equity.

___ 6. Equal sacrifice typically requires that higher-income groups pay larger dollar amounts of taxes.

___ 7. Taxes reduce individuals' ability to command resources.

___ 8. Under tax financing, the resources released and made available to government as a result of the taxes typically correspond to the resources needed to undertake the collectively chosen government activities.

___ 9. Direct appropriation or acquisition of resources allows government to have the correct resources released and made available to it.

___ 10. An excise tax is a selective tax.

___ 11. In a progressive tax rate structure, the average tax rate eventually exceeds the marginal tax rate.

___ 12. The retail sales tax is generally characterized by a regressive tax rate structure applied to the consumption base.

___ 13. The goals of efficiency and equity in the distribution of taxes among citizens are unlikely to conflict.

___ 14. Tax avoidance is illegal.

___ 15. Tax avoidance distorts consumer choices.

___ 16. The use of debt to finance capital projects can improve the efficiency of the use of resources.

___ 17. Voluntary donations are a more viable financing tool in communities where individuals have differing tastes and goals.

___ 18. User charges are typically less than the average cost of providing the good or service.

___ 19. The markup on liquor by government-operated stores is equivalent to a tax on liquor.

___ 20. Future capital costs involved in expanding capacity can be considered as long-run marginal costs in evaluating the pricing of a congestible public good.

_____ 21. Evidence suggests that lotteries are a regressive tax when expressed as a percent of the income of those who play them.

Multiple Choice Questions: Choose the best answer.

 _____ 1. The method of financing government activity can affect the:
   a) political equilibrium.
   b) overall market equilibrium. ⁴
   c) efficiency with which resources are employed in private uses. ⁴
   d) distribution of income. ⁴
   e) all of the above.

_____ 2. The argument that the means of financing government-supplied goods and services should be linked to the benefits that citizens receive from government is called the:
   a) efficiency principle.
   b) benefit principle.
   c) ability-to-pay principle.
   d) law of equitable distribution.

_____ 3. Which of the following does not constitute an argument in favor of using the benefit principle?
   a) most government-provided goods and services result in collectively consumed benefits.
   b) the benefit principle links the cost per unit of government-provided services with the marginal benefits of those services.
   c) the jurisdiction in question is a small, homogeneous community.
   d) the benefits from government-provided services are highly correlated with a particular economic activity.

 _____ 4. The ability-to-pay principle:
   a) maintains that taxes should be distributed according to the capacity of taxpayers to pay them.
   b) views tax shares independent of the individual marginal benefits of government activity.
   c) requires a collective agreement regarding an equity criterion.
   d) all of the above.

 _____ 5. When individuals of differing economic capacity pay tax bills which differ according to some collectively chosen notion of fairness, the tax system achieves:
   a) economic efficiency.
   b) horizontal equity.
   c) vertical equity.
   d) utility maximization.
   e) all of the above.

D 6. Taxes:
   a) are compulsory payments associated with certain activities.
   b) reallocate resources from private to government use.
   c) often cause relative prices to change.
   d) all of the above.

C/E 7. A tax which taxes all of the components of an economic base, with no exclusions, exemptions, or deductions is:
   a) an excise tax.
   b) a selective tax.
   c) a general tax.
   d) equitable.
   e) none of the above.

Flat tax = general or head tax

D 8. If for all values of the tax base the average tax rate is equal to the marginal tax rate, the tax rate structure is termed:
   a) efficient.
   b) regressive.
   c) progressive.
   d) proportional.
   e) equitable.

A 9. Which of the following is most crucial in determining behavior changes that can cause losses in efficiency?
   a) the marginal tax rate.
   b) the average tax rate.
   c) the degree of progressivity.
   d) the number of tax brackets.

E 10. The retail sales tax is:
   a) an excise tax.
   b) regressive with respect to the consumption base.
   c) regressive with respect to the income base.
   d) both a and b.
   e) both a and c.

D 11. The criteria for evaluating alternative means of government finance include which of the following?
   a) efficiency.
   b) administrative ease.
   c) equity.
   d) all of the above.

B 12. Noncompliance with the tax laws by failing to pay taxes that are due is called:
   a) criminal avoidance.
   b) tax evasion.
   c) tax avoidance.
   d) tax exemption.

____ 13. Which of the following would be expected to increase tax evasion?
   a) lower tax rates.
   b) increased penalties for tax evasion.
   c) a decrease in the proportion of tax forms audited.
   d) an increase in the number of IRS field agents.

____ 14. Which of the following is the best candidate for debt finance?
   a) food stamps.
   b) a new fire truck.
   c) a new hospital.
   d) an increased number of IRS auditors.

____ 15. The effect of increased government borrowing on the price level is dependent upon:
   a) the maturity structure of government debt.
   b) the effect of the bargain on the velocity of circulation of money.
   c) the extent to which the monetary reserves are increased by the central bank.
   d) all of the above.

____ 16. Which of the following statements about user charges is false?
   a) They are prices determined through market interaction.
   b) They can only finance government supplied goods and services when excludability is possible.
   c) They force individuals to compare some of the benefits of using public services with the costs imposed by the user charge.
   d) They ration the use of public facilities.

____ 17. Which of the following is an example of a user charge?
   a) an admission fee to a public museum.
   b) a toll on a superhighway.
   c) a building permit fee.
   d) the fare on a commuter train.
   e) all of the above.

____ 18. The appropriate user charge for a government-supplied good or service:
   a) is independent of any external benefits.
   b) is zero for all congestible goods or services.
   c) should be equal to the marginal social cost of accomodating an additional user.
   d) will fully cover the cost of providing the good or service.

____ 19. Which of the following is not an example of a government enterprise?
   a) a state liquor store.
   b) a government lottery.
   c) a municipal utility.
   d) a state prison.

20. In the United States, there is a general consensus that ability to pay varies with:
    a) consumption.
    b) income.
    c) real property.
    d) holdings of stocks and bonds.

Short Answer Questions: Answer in the space provided.

1. List an example of a tax levied on consumption, a tax levied on income, and a tax levied on wealth. What is the tax rate structure of each of these taxes? If these are selective taxes, please note how the tax base is restricted and/or any deductions or exemptions which are part of the tax.

2. List three examples of user charges. Why are user charges effective in financing these government activities? Do these user charges fully finance this government activity? Why or why not?

Problems: Be sure to show your work.

1. Table 10.1 in your textbook presents a progressive tax rate structure. Using this structure, calculate the total tax bill, marginal tax rate, and average tax rate for a taxpayer with an income of $37,000. How would your answers change if the person's income increased to $250,000? In deciding how many hours to work, which tax rate is most relevant?

2. The cost of constructing a five-mile highway is $5 million. The demand for road services in vehicles per mile per hour is given by $Q = 5200 - 2P$. Congestion begins when traffic on the road reaches 1000 vehicles per mile per hour. The marginal social cost of congestion is $1 for the 1001st vehicle and increases by one dollar with each subsequent vehicle.

   a) What is the efficient level of traffic in this situation?

   b) What user charge would reduce traffic to this efficient level?

SKETCH ANSWERS TO CHAPTER 10

Issue in Brief:

1. Compare your answers with those of your classmates.

2. Competitors include horse racing, dog racing, jai alai, casinos, bingo parlors, and sweepstakes.

3. The Indian Gaming Regulatory Act of 1988.

True/False:

1. F They accounted for about 75 percent of revenue.
2. T
3. T
4. F They must be taxed according to their marginal benefits.
5. T
6. T
7. T
8. F They do not generally correspond.
9. T
10. T
11. F The marginal tax rate exceeds the average tax rate.
12. F It is characterized by a proportional tax rate structure.
13. F They are likely to conflict.
14. F Tax evasion is illegal.
15. T
16. T
17. F They are more viable where individuals have similar tastes and goals.
18. T
19. T
20. T
21. T

Multiple Choice:

1. e	6. d	11. d	16. a
2. b	7. c	12. b	17. e
3. a	8. d	13. c	18. c
4. d	9. a	14. c	19. d
5. c	10. e	15. d	20. b

Short Answer:

1. Compare your answers with those of your classmates. An example of a consumption tax would be an admissions tax at an amusement park. This would be a selective tax in that only admissions to a certain form of entertainment are taxed. A personal income tax is an example of an income

tax. It is a progressive tax in the United States and is selective due to its numerous exemptions and deductions. The real property tax is levied on wealth and is generally a proportional tax. It is selective in that only real property is taxed (and not even all real property) and there are exemptions such as the homestead exemption.

2. Compare your answers with those of your classmates. Water and sewer service fees are an example of a user charge which can fully finance the activity upon which it is levied. User charges are effective here due to the price-excludable nature of water and sewer services, as well as the ability to objectively measure water and sewer use/benefits. Building permits are not likely to fully finance building inspections and the like due to the external benefits from building permits. User charges for building permits attempt to capture some of the costs of government services related to new building (for example, health inspections). A third example of a user charge is a pool admission fee. The pool represents a price-excludable congestible public good and is thus a good candidate for a user charge. The user charge is unlikely to fully finance the pool due to the upfront capital costs and the problems created by congestion.

Problems:

1. The taxpayer with a $37,000 income will pay $5750 in taxes. The marginal tax rate is 25% and the average tax rate is (5750/37,000) = 15.54%. The taxpayer with a $250,000 income will pay $77,000 in taxes. The marginal tax rate is 35% and the average tax rate is 30.8%. The marginal tax rate is the most relevant in decisions as to the work/leisure choice.

2.

   a) $Q^* = 2400$. (remember to set MSB equal to MSC)

   b) optimal charge = $1400 per vehicle per mile.

Chapter Recap: You should now be able to answer the following questions:

1. How does the means of finance affect important economic and political variables?

2. Compare and contrast the benefit and ability-to-pay principles of government finance.

3. Compare and contrast the notions of horizontal and vertical equity.

4. Discuss the basic principles of taxation and tax structure. Be sure to discuss the notions of the tax base, tax rate, and the various types of tax rate structures.

5. Carefully outline the basic criteria for evaluating alternative methods of government finance.

6. Contrast tax evasion and tax avoidance.

7. Discuss the nature and use of nontax means of government finance.

8. How can congestible government-supplied services and the products of government enterprises be appropriately priced?

CHAPTER 11

Taxation, Prices, Efficiency, and the Distribution of Income

Chapter Objectives: After reading and working through this chapter, you should understand:

1. The notion of a lump-sum tax and its use as a benchmark for analyzing the effects of price-distorting taxes including the excess burden of taxation.

2. The concepts of unit and ad valorem taxes, and their effects on market equilibrium.

3. The incidence of unit and ad valorem taxes, including the concept of tax shifting.

4. Multimarket analysis of tax incidence.

5. The notions of budget, expenditure, and differential tax incidence.

6. The use of the Lorenz Curve and Gini coefficient in evaluating the distribution of income in an economy.

Chapter Summary:

1. This chapter analyzes how taxes on goods and services affect market equilibrium prices and quantities as well as the well-being of taxpayers.

2. A *lump-sum* tax is a fixed sum that a person would pay per year independent of any controllable variable. Such taxes have only income effects and do not distort economic choices. Nevertheless, lump-sum taxes generally affect the distribution of income. A *price-distorting tax* is one that causes the net price received by sellers of a good or service to diverge from the gross price paid by buyers. The loss in well-being due to the use of a price-distorting tax rather than a lump-sum tax is called the *excess burden of taxation*. The loss in well-being to the taxpayer is the individual excess burden of taxation. The *total excess burden of a tax* refers to the loss in net benefits from private use of resources that results from the economic inefficiency introduced by a price-distorting tax.

3. A *unit excise tax* is a levy of a fixed amount per unit of a good exchanged in a market. Such a tax is a price-distorting tax which results in a deadweight loss. The excess burden of a unit tax varies quadratically with the size of the tax and increases with greater price elasticity of demand or supply. *An ad valorem tax* is levied as a percentage of the price of a good or service and is also a distortionary tax. Again, the excess burden varies with the square of the tax rate and increases with more price-elastic supply or demand.

4. The *incidence of a tax* is the distribution of the burden of paying it. The transfer of the burden of paying a tax away from those who are legally liable for it is called the *shifting of a tax*. Taxes may be shifted forward from sellers to buyers or backward from buyers to sellers. Tax incidence is generally analyzed through calculation of tax-induced price changes in the good or service in question. The burden of a tax is dependent upon the relative price elasticities of supply and demand for the taxed good or service. *Ceteris paribus*, the more inelastic the supply the greater the portion of the tax borne by sellers. Crucially, the burden of a tax is independent of the legal liability for paying the tax!

5. The effects of a tax are unlikely to be limited to a single market. There are likely to be repercussions in related markets and additional feedback effects to the market initially taxed. It is difficult, but nonetheless important, to try to trace out these effects through the economy. Such analysis must consider both input and output markets.

6. The efficiency loss of a price-distorting tax system can be reduced by means of tax rate adjustments. In general, efficiency loss can be minimized if goods are taxed at rates that decreased with the elasticity of demand such that the percentage reduction in quantity demanded due to the substitution effect of the tax-induced price increase is equal across goods.

7. The incidence of a specific government policy refers to the resulting change in the distribution of income available for private use attributable to that policy. Effective incidence analysis requires one to hold all variables other than the specific policy variables constant. Budget incidence, expenditure incidence, and differential tax incidence are three analytical frameworks within which the effects of government policy are analyzed. *Budget incidence* evaluates the combined effects of expenditure and tax policies. *Expenditure analysis* evaluates the differential effect of expenditure policies. *Differential tax analysis* evaluates the differential effect of tax policies.

8. A *Lorenz Curve* plots information on the distribution of income by size brackets. The *Gini coefficient* uses the information in the Lorenz Curve to measure income inequality by calculating the ratio of the area between the curve and the line of equal distribution to the total area beneath the line of equal distribution. The smaller the coefficient, the more equal the distribution. The Lorenz Curve and Gini coefficient provide rough measures of income inequality.

9. A number of empirical studies of the United States tax system have concluded that the system as a whole is only mildly progressive, but federal taxes remain progressive even in the face of recent tax law changes. The robustness of these results is somewhat questionable due to the lack of solid multimarket evidence and imprecise estimates of relevant elasticities. Evidence on tax shifting of property taxes, corporate income taxes, retail sales taxes, and payroll taxes remains contradictory and sparse, with continuing controversy revolving around these issues.

Issue in Brief: Taxes, the Family, and Education

In 1997, under the guide of "middle-income family tax relief," the Congress passed the "Taxpayer Relief Act of 1997." A key feature of the new law is a tax credit to families with cheldren. There is also a tax credit for college tuition expenses. These new credits are available mainly to lower and middle-income families because the benefits are phased out as income increases according to a complex formula. The maximum credit is $500 per child which is directly deducted from the family's tax liability. Couples with more than $110,000 adjusted gross income and single parents with more than $75,000 adjusted gross income (based on 1997 income) receive lower credits. For college tuition a tax credit of $1,500 per year is available for the first two years of college with additional credits of up to $1000 per year for each additional year of higher education. Eligibility for these credits and the cash amounts are phased out as adjusted gross income rises above $80,000 for married taxpayers and $50,000 for single parents.

Questions for Discussion:

1. How can the tax credits be regarded as subsidies? What affect will the tax credits have on resource allocation?

2. What is the likely incidence of the tax credits?

CHAPTER REVIEW QUESTIONS

True/False Questions: If false, explain how to correct the statement to make it true.

____ 1. A tax on any good or service affects incentives to buy and sell that item.

____ 2. A lump-sum tax does not affect consumption, saving, or investment.

____ 3. A head tax would necessarily be regressive with respect to income.

____ 4. A price-distorting tax creates a wedge between the price received by sellers and the price paid by buyers.

___ 5. The excess burden of taxation is measured by the income effect of a price-distorting tax.

___ 6. A <u>unit</u> tax varies with the price of the taxed good or service.

___ 7. The excess burden of a price-distorting tax can be recovered through appropriate distribution of the tax revenues.

___ 8. Excess burden varies proportionately with the size of a <u>unit</u> tax.

___ 9. Assuming that income effects are negligible, a tax on any commodity which has either a price elasticity of demand or price elasticity of supply equal to zero has a zero efficiency loss.

___ 10. The efficiency-loss ratio measures the excess burden per dollar of tax revenue.

___ 11. Taxes on capital income have been reduced substantially from the levels that prevailed in 1973.

___ 12. Researchers have concluded that the efficiency losses caused by taxes in the United States are small relative to the amount of revenue collected.

___ 13. When a tax is shifted, those legally liable for paying the tax incur losses.

___ 14. The retail sales tax is an ad valorem tax.

___ 15. Workers base their work-leisure choices on the gross wage.

___ 16. The final incidence of a tax is independent of whether the tax is collected from buyers or sellers of goods and services.

___ 17. A unit tax on a good whose price elasticity of demand is zero would have a positive excess burden.

___ 18. *Ceteris paribus*, a monopoly will shift more of a unit tax to consumers than would a competitive industry.

___ 19. The effect of a tax in any one market is not likely to be confined to that market alone.

___ 20. Lorenz Curve analysis does not pick up households who trade places in the income distribution.

___ 21. If the Gini coefficient is lower for a post-tax distribution of income, this is evidence that the tax has reduced income inequality.

_____ 22. A study of the incidence of the overall 1980 tax structure in the United States concluded that, for the most part, the distribution of the tax burden is roughly proportional to income.

_____ 23. The lump-sum tax introduced in Britain was very popular.

_____ 24. Recent tax reforms have increased the progressivity of the U.S. tax system.

Multiple Choice Questions: Choose the best answer.

1. When taxes are reflected in the prices of goods and services traded in competitive markets in which there are no externalities:
   a) the income effect will outweigh the substitution effect.
   b) the substitution effect will outweigh the income effect.
   c) losses in efficiency are likely to result.
   d) none of the above.

2. Lump-sum taxes:
   a) have only income effects.
   b) have both income and substitution effects.
   c) have only substitution effects.
   d) vary with consumer income.

re-read lump sum taxes

3. Which of the following statements is false?
   a) lump-sum taxes are likely to affect the distribution of income.
   b) lump-sum taxes prevent prices from equalling the marginal social cost and benefit of goods and services.
   c) lump-sum taxes are not tied to any controllable variable.
   d) the marginal tax rate associated with a lump-sum tax is always zero.

4. A tax which causes the net price received by sellers of a good or service to diverge from the gross price paid by buyers is called:
   a) a lump-sum tax.
   b) an ad valorem tax.
   c) a unit excise tax.
   d) a price-distorting tax.

5. Which of the following would be an example of a lump-sum tax?
   a) a head tax.
   b) a retail sales tax.
   c) a personal income tax.
   d) a passport fee.
   user fees

6. With conventionally shaped supply and demand curves, which of the following represents the correct ranking from lowest to highest of the prices which will prevail in the face of a unit excise tax?
   a) net post-tax price, gross post-tax price, original equilibrium price.
   b) original equilibrium price, net post-tax price, gross post-tax price.
   c) gross post-tax price, original equilibrium price, net post-tax price.
   d) net post-tax price, original equilibrium price, gross post-tax price.
   e) none of the above.

7. The loss in well-being caused by the substitution effect of a price-distorting tax is called:
   a) disutility.
   b) diminishing marginal utility.
   c) excess burden.
   d) diminishing marginal substitutability.

8. Which of the following is a unit excise tax?
   a) a retail sales tax of $.05 on each dollar of purchases.
   b) an admissions tax of $1.00 on each ticket purchased.
   c) an income tax of $.30 on each dollar earned.
   d) the Social Security payroll tax.

9. A unit excise tax collected from sellers:
   a) decreases the marginal cost of selling the product.
   b) increases the marginal cost of selling the product.
   c) increases the marginal benefit of consuming the product.
   d) none of the above.

10. Excess burden:
    a) represents the loss in well-being due to the substitution effect of a tax.
    b) is a deadweight loss.
    c) varies with the amount of a unit tax.
    d) all of the above.

11. Which of the following results in a larger excess burden, *ceteris paribus*?
    a) a smaller unit tax.
    b) less elastic demand with respect to price.
    c) more elastic supply with respect to price.
    d) a smaller pretax quantity.

12. *Ceteris paribus*, a tax on which of the following is likely to be most efficient?
    a) hot dogs.
    b) aspirin.
    c) insulin.
    d) automobiles.

13. The efficiency-loss ratio of a tax is equal to:
    a) excess burden/tax revenue.
    b) excess burden/pre-tax quantity.
    c) unit tax/utility loss.
    d) excess burden/utility loss.

14. Ballard, Shoven, and Whalley found that taxes on which of the following caused the greatest distortion in 1973?
    a) labor income.
    b) Social Security.
    c) interest and investment income.
    d) corporate profits and capital gains.

15. Transfer of tax burden from buyers who are liable for its payment to sellers through a decrease in the market price of the taxed good is called:
    a) tax evasion.
    b) backward shifting.
    c) forward shifting.
    d) deadweight loss.

16. Which of the following is an ad valorem tax?   *valve added*
    a) a retail sales tax of .05 on each dollar of purchases.
    b) an admissions tax of $1.00 on each ticket purchased.
    c) a fee of $5.00 on each building permit filed.
    d) a road tax of $500 on each automobile owned.

17. The final incidence of a tax:
    a) is generally borne by the buyer of a good or service.
    b) is generally borne by the seller of a good or service.
    c) requires knowledge of the legal liability for the tax.
    d) is independent of the legal liability for the tax.
    e) both a and c.

18. *Ceteris paribus*, which of the following values of the price elasticity of supply will result in the greatest portion of the tax being borne by buyers?
    a) 0
    b) 0.5
    c) 1.5
    d) an infinite price elasticity of supply.

19. If demand for a good or service were perfectly inelastic with respect to price:
    a) sellers would bear the entire burden of a unit tax on the commodity.
    b) buyers would bear the entire burden of a unit tax on the commodity.
    c) the burden of a unit tax on the commodity would be shared by buyers and sellers.
    d) none of the above.

20. Evaluating the effects of both government expenditure and tax policies on the distribution of income in the private sector involves the analysis of:
    a) expenditure incidence.
    b) tax incidence.
    c) budget incidence.
    d) none of the above.

21. The Lorenz Curve:
    a) requires knowledge of the percentage of households ranked in terms of their income.
    b) contains a line of equal distribution.
    c) allows comparison of income distributions.
    d) all of the above.

22. Which of the following measures the degree of inequality for any income distribution?
    a) Lorenz Curve.
    b) Gini coefficient.
    c) the index of income inequality.
    d) all of the above.

23. Empirical evidence indicates that distribution of federal taxes in the United States is:
    a) progressive.
    b) proportional.
    c) mildly regressive.
    d) significantly regressive.

Short Answer Questions: Answer in the space provided.

1. List three price-distorting taxes on items you purchase or sell. How have these taxes affected your economic behavior?

2. Offer an example of a tax which is forward shifted and one which is backward shifted. Be sure to note who has typically been found to bear the burden of the tax.

Problems: Be sure to show your work.

1. Do Problem 1 in your textbook. Now assume that the $1-per-gallon tax is levied on the price paid by buyers. Redo the problem using this new information.

2. If the annual demand for liquor in Problem 1 was given by Qd = 500,000, how would your answers change? Why?

SKETCH ANSWERS TO CHAPTER 11

Issue in Brief:

1. The tax credits will lower the cost of both child-rearing and college for eligible parents—this will subsidize both child rearing and education and could increase the birth rate and increase the demand for educational services, possible beyond the efficient levels. However, insofar as there are externalities associated with college education, some of this excess burden could be offset.

2. Because the benefits are phased out as income rises, the incidence is likely to be progressive with respect to income.

True/False:

1. T
2. F   Consumption, saving, and investment may be reduced, but in a non-distortionary fashion.
3. T
4. T
5. F   It is measured by the substitution effect.
6. F   It is a fixed amount per unit, independent of the price.
7. F   It is a deadweight loss which cannot be recovered.
8. F   It actually varies more than proportionately.
9. T
10. T
11. T
12. F   The losses are substantial.
13. F   Those legally liable gain from shifting.
14. T
15. F   These choices are based upon the net wage.
16. T
17. F   There would be no excess burden.
18. F   A monopoly would shift less of the tax.
19. T
20. T
21. T
22. T
23. F   It was very unpopular.
24. T

Multiple Choice:

1. c	6. d	11. c	16. a	21. d
2. a	7. c	12. c	17. d	22. b
3. b	8. b	13. a	18. d	23. a
4. d	9. b	14. c	19. b	
5. a	10. d	15. b	20. c	

Short Answer:

1. Compare your answers with those of your classmates. Concentrate on how the taxes alter the relative prices and alter the attractiveness of substitute and complementary goods and services.

2. The retail sales tax is generally thought to be forward shifted to consumers. Payroll taxes, like social security taxes, on employers are generally thought to be backward shifted to workers. These are just sample answers. Compare your answers with those of your classmates.

Problems:

1. The demand curve now shifts vertically downward by the amount of the tax ($1). See Figure 12.4 in your textbook for an example of this type of shift. The rest of your answers should be the same as in the original problem, because tax incidence is independent of the legal liability for the tax. Check figure: post-tax quantity is 288,000 gallons.

2. Demand is now perfectly inelastic. Pre-tax equilibrium price is $16.67, and the corresponding quantity is 500,000. Post-tax, the quantity would remain at 500,000 and the net price at $16.67. Buyers would bear the entire burden of the tax and pay a gross price of $17.67. There will be no excess burden since there is no change in quantity.

Chapter Recap: You should now be able to answer the following questions:

1. What is a lump-sum tax? How is it used as a benchmark for analyzing the effects of price-distorting taxes?

2. Compare and contrast unit and ad valorem taxes. Compare their effects on market equilibrium.

3. Describe graphically the incidence of unit and ad valorem taxes. How is tax shifting illustrated in your graphs?

4. What is multimarket analysis of tax incidence? Why is it important?

5. Describe the use of the Lorenz Curve and Gini coefficient in evaluating the distribution of income in an economy.

APPENDIX TO CHAPTER 11

The Excess Burden of Taxation: Technical Analysis

Appendix Objectives: After reading and working through this appendix, you should understand:

1. The derivation of major excess burden formulas.

2. The nature and use of compensated demand and supply curves.

APPENDIX REVIEW QUESTIONS

Short Answer Questions: Answer in the space provided.

1. Derive the formula for the excess burden of a unit tax.

2. What is a compensated demand curve? What can it be used for?

3. What is a compensated supply curve?

SKETCH ANSWERS TO APPENDIX REVIEW QUESTIONS

Short Answer:

1. See the first section of the appendix text.

2. A compensated demand curve shows the relationship between price and quantity demanded with all income effects eliminated. It is especially useful for isolating the excess burden of taxes in instances where income effects are not negligible. In general, a compensated demand curve is less elastic than a regular demand curve.

3. A compensated supply curve expresses the relationship between price and quantity supplied with all income effects removed. Compensated supply curves tend to be more elastic than their regular counterparts.

CHAPTER 12

Budget Deficits and the Government Debt

Chapter Objectives: After reading and working through this chapter, you should understand:

1. The nature and various definitions of budget deficits.

2. The general history of government budget deficits and debt finance in the United States.

3. The economic effects of budget deficits and the way these effects depend on the level of government at which the deficit is incurred.

4. The role of government debt as a finance tool in the United States.

5. The various types of government debt and their differing economic implications.

6. The effects of economic fluctuations on the value of government debt.

7. The unique issues confronted in debt finance by state and local governments.

Chapter Summary:

1. This chapter investigates both the current and the future impact of budget deficits and increased government debt on the well-being of citizens. It analyzes the causes of budget deficits and their effects on interest rates, future tax rates, and private production. The chapter compares and contrasts the use of debt finance by the federal government and by state and local governments.

2. A *budget deficit* is the excess of government expenditures over revenues raised by taxes, fees, and charges. The size of the budget deficit in any given year is influenced by economic fluctuations. The *high-employment deficit* estimates the budget deficit which would prevail at a designated level of unemployment in the economy. A structural deficit represents a basic

imbalance between government expenditures and revenues, persisting even in the face of high employment in the economy.

3. Up to 1998 federal budget has officially been in deficit every year since 1970. The deficit increased sharply in the early 1980s, began to shrink in the late 1980s, and has again increased in recent years, especially relative to government expenditures and GDP. In 1998 thanks to a booming economy and legislation enacted by Congress in 1990 and 1997, the federal government was running a budget surplus for the first time in nearly 20 years. The Budget Act of 1997 requires a balanced budget in 2002. However, later in the 21st century, because of aging of the population there are likely to be pressures to use deficit finance again to avoid tax increases.

4. Budget deficits are basically eliminated through tax or fee increases or through reduced government spending. Neither choice is politically popular and the costs and benefits of such actions are unclear and controversial. One major issue is the extent to which defense and nondefense programs should share in any budget cuts.

5. The economic effects of budget deficits are controversial. A federal budget deficit adds to the national debt and increases the future interest costs to the federal government. In 1997, the federal government allocated 14 percent of its expenditures to paying interest on its debt. The traditional view of federal government budget deficits hypothesizes that, by increasing the demand for loanable funds, the federal government's financing of the deficit increases interest rates and crowds out interest-sensitive private sector expenditures. By crowding out investment, the nation's real rate of growth is retarded.

6. Alternatively, the Ricardian view of government deficits envisions citizens with the foresight to realize that increased government debt due to deficits translates into higher taxes in the future. In anticipation of these taxes, as well as because of the increased current purchasing power under debt rather than tax finance, citizens increase their savings. This increase in savings increases the supply of loanable funds and offsets (or helps to offset) the increased demand for loanable funds. This reduces or eliminates any increase in the interest rate as a result of government deficits. If an increase in government borrowing to finance a deficit sufficiently increases private saving so that interest rates remain fixed, *Ricardian equivalence* prevails. Economists subscribing to the Ricardian view have also suggested that the current generation will increase bequests in an effort to offset the future taxes on their heirs brought about by debt finance.

7. The net contribution of the government sector to national saving is determined by the combined surplus or deficit of government budgets at all levels of government. Large federal deficits have contributed to a significant decrease in national saving since about 1980. Such a reduced supply of savings can contribute to increased real interest rates and lower levels of economic growth. A budget surplus in 1998 will add to national saving.

8. *Gross federal debt* includes all federal debt including that owed to government agencies, trust funds, and the Federal Reserve Banks. It amounted to more than $5 trillion in 1997, or about 65 percent of GDP. The *net federal debt* is that portion of the federal government debt which is held by the public. Net federal debt has significantly increased over earlier years and accounted for about 50% of GDP as of 1997. Given these magnitudes, as well as the advantages of using debt finance for certain types of expenditures, it is not feasible or advisable to extinguish the national debt.

9. The portion of a government's indebtedness owed to its own citizens is called *internal debt*. Repayment of internal debt involves no loss in resources to the economy. Instead, it redistributes purchasing power from taxpayers to fellow citizens who are bondholders. *External debt* is held by economic actors outside the government's jurisdiction. Its repayment results in a loss in resources to the economy to the economy of the borrowing government. The bulk of United States federal debt is internal debt, but in recent years the proportion of external debt has increased with a strong dollar and high interest rates, not to mention balance-of-trade deficits.

10. The government deficit can be adjusted to take account of inflation, as well as for the effects of inflation and changing interest rates on the market value of outstanding net debt. Including the inflation tax as part of government revenues, and accounting for the reduced market value of outstanding net debt that results when interest rates rise, can result in an adjusted government deficit which is much smaller than the officially reported value. Much recent research has focused on this particular issue. Similarly, the projected Social Security trust fund surpluses have raised issues regarding their appropriate treatment in government accounting.

11. Perhaps the biggest difference between the use of debt by the federal government and by state and local governments is the basically unrestricted revenue-generating capability of the federal government, which makes the risk of default on federal securities essentially zero. In addition, state and local governments are basically price-takers in the market for funds, with variations from the risk-free interest rate essentially a function of the debt ratings provided by private rating services. Bonds backed by the taxing power of the issuing jurisdiction are called *general obligation bonds*, while those backed by the promise of revenue on the funded project are called *revenue bonds*. Due to their lower perceived risk, general obligation bonds usually carry a lower interest rate than do revenue bonds.

12. Due to the mobility of their populations, state and local governments often find debt financing to be an attractive way of matching the costs and benefits of public projects. Debt finance also makes collective choices involving long-term projects more attractive, since voters will not bear the concentrated costs of immediate tax financing. Unfortunately, most of the debt of these jurisdictions is external debt and carries with it the loss of resources that results when such debt is repaid.

13. The *burden of the debt* is the redistributive effect of debt financing. There is some disagreement about who bears the burden of government debt. Many argue that the burden is not borne by the current generation since the purchase of government securities is voluntary and presumably utility enhancing. Instead, the burden falls on those who must pay taxes in order to finance interest payments and retirement of the debt. The bequest effect discussed above may help to offset this burden on future generations. Also, it should be remembered that the benefits of capital projects flow to future generations and should help to offset the costs of repaying the debt used to finance such projects.

Issue in Brief: The Budget Balance: Surplus to Deficit?

In fiscal year 1998 for the first time since 1970 the federal budget will have a surplus. The Budget Act of 1997 required that the federal budget be in balance by the year 2002, however, that deadline was beat four years in advance. The Budget Enforcement Act of 1990 put caps on spending for defense, international, and domestic spending and required that new spending programs or specific tax cuts be enacted only if other taxes are increased or other spending is cut. However, later in the 21st century it is likely that aging of the population will increase government spending and could course deficit finance to once again be tempting to the Congress.

Questions for Discussion:

1. List the factors that affect the size of the federal budget deficit or surplus in any given year and then examine information on the performance of the U.S. economy in 1998 to explain why the goal of a balanced budget was met in advance of the date scheduled.

2. Read the information on aging of the population in Chapter 1 and in the Chapter on Social Security in the textbook and explain why the budget deficit could become a problem later on in the 21st century.

CHAPTER REVIEW QUESTIONS

True/False Questions: If false, explain how to correct the statement to make it true.

____ 1. If federal budget deficits recur, the national debt will continue to increase.

____ 2. The deficits of the 1980s cannot be regarded as structural.

____ 3. According to the CBO, changes in the unadjusted budget deficit as a percent of GDP provide a good indication of the burden of deficit finance on the public.

____ 4. In recent years, federal government budget deficits in the United States have been incurred to stabilize the economy.

____ 5. The Budget Act of 1997 provisions require a balanced budget by fiscal year 2002.

____ 6. High interest rates contribute to a lower federal budget deficit.

____ 7. The budget deficit varies with the level of economic activity in a given year.

____ 8. Calculation of the high-employment deficit requires that a benchmark level of unemployment be subjectively and arbitrarily selected.

____ 9. According to the traditional view, a federal budget deficit has no effect on interest rates.

____ 10. The Ricardian view of government deficits argues that people perceive the increased future tax burden that results from the use of debt finance.

____ 11. The debt of the federal government is more than three times that of all state and local governments combined.

____ 12. United States securities held by Federal Reserve Banks are part of the gross federal debt.

____ 13. It would take less than one year of federal government spending at its current level to retire the national debt in full.

____ 14. The net federal debt is mainly owed to United States firms and citizens.

____ 15. Repayment of external debt involves no outflow of resources.

____ 16. Increased interest rates reduce the real market value of outstanding government debt.

____ 17. Social Security trust fund surpluses decrease negative saving by the federal government.

____ 18. State and local debt issues are inherently less risky than those of the federal government.

____ 19. Generally, a higher proportion of a state or local government's debt is internal as compared with that of the federal government.

_____ 20. Many state and local governments have capital budgets that involve projects financed exclusively by public borrowing.

_____ 21. Debt finance results in income redistribution.

_____ 22. The burden of debt on future generations cannot be offset.

_____ 23. Debt finance can result in "pay-as-you-use" finance, better linking the costs and benefits of government projects.

Multiple Choice Questions: Choose the best answer.

_____ 1. From 1970 – 1997, federal budget deficits:
  a) have been incurred deliberately to stabilize the economy.
  b) can be regarded as structural.
  c) have continuously increased as a percentage of GDP.
  d) all of the above.

_____ 2. A government budget deficit can adversely affect a nation's balance of international trade through:
  a) higher real interest rates.
  b) upward pressure on the nation's exchange rate.
  c) its influence on disposable income.
  d) all of the above.

_____ 3. Which of the following statements is true?
  a) A budget deficit adds to national saving.
  b) A budget deficit decreases national saving.
  c) A budget deficit will decreases interest rates.
  d) A budget surplus will reduce national saving.

_____ 4. The Budget Act of 1997 mandates a balanced federal budget:
  a) immediately.
  b) by fiscal year 2002.
  c) by fiscal year 2025.
  d) but has no target date.

_____ 5. Eliminating a budget deficit requires:
  a) increased borrowing.
  b) cuts in defense spending.
  c) cuts in nondefense spending.
  d) decreased taxes.
  e) either reduced government spending or increased taxes.

____ 6. Which of the following contributed to the growth of the federal budget deficit in the early 1980s?
   a) reduced federal tax rates.
   b) an accelerated buildup of national defense expenditures.
   c) the growth of entitlement programs.
   d) all of the above.

____ 7. The budget deficit that would prevail at a designated low level of unemployment in the economy is called:
   a) the cyclical deficit.
   b) the high-employment deficit.
   c) the natural deficit rate.
   d) none of the above.

____ 8. The view that federal government budget deficits contribute to higher interest rates is part of:
   a) the traditional view of deficits.
   b) the Ricardian view of deficits.
   c) the asset-substitution effect.
   d) the bequest effect.

____ 9. High real interest rates:
   a) crowd out interest-sensitive expenditures.
   b) decrease job opportunities.
   c) contribute to lagging worker productivity.
   d) increase the demand for the domestic currency by foreigners.
   e) all of the above.

____ 10. The Ricardian view of government deficits argues:
   a) that the future tax burden imposed by debt finance will be ignored.
   b) that the private sector supply of loanable funds will increase in the face of government deficits.
   c) taxpayers are less capable of saving when debt finance is used rather than tax finance.
   d) that government deficits reduce interest rates.

____ 11. The portion of the debt of the federal government held by the general public, excluding the holdings of United States government agencies, trust funds, and the Federal Reserve Banks is called:
   a) the gross federal debt.
   b) the net public interest.
   c) the net federal debt.
   d) the level of public indebtedness.

_____ 12. The net federal debt in 1996 amounted to about what percent of GDP?
  a) 25.
  b) 50.
  c) 75.
  d) 100.

_____ 13. The portion of a government's indebtedness owed to its own citizens is:
  a) external debt.
  b) internal debt.
  c) not recoverable.
  d) net debt.

_____ 14. External debt:
  a) involves an outflow of resources when repaid.
  b) varies in importance with changes in the interest rate.
  c) represents about one-fifth of the net outstanding U.S. debt.
  d) has grown rapidly in the United States since 1970.
  e) all of the above.

_____ 15. Which of the following decreases the real market value of the net federal debt?
  a) inflation.
  b) decreased interest rates.
  c) increased federal deficits.
  d) none of the above.

_____ 16. State and local debt issues:
  a) generally have lower risk of default than federal issues.
  b) are evaluated by private bond-rating services.
  c) carry interest rates which are independent of the jurisdiction's past repayment history.
  d) affect the interest rate in the market for loanable funds.

_____ 17. Debt issues backed by the taxing power of the issuing jurisdiction are called:
  a) treasury warrants.
  b) government securities.
  c) revenue bonds.
  d) general obligation bonds.

_____ 18. Debt finance:
  a) postpones the burden of taxation to future taxpayers.
  b) does not require compulsion in the sale of its instruments.
  c) allows collective approval for projects that will benefit future citizens who are not present in the jurisdiction to vote at the time of project approval.
  d) all of the above.

___ 19. Which of the following statements about the burden of the debt is false?
   a) It represents the redistributive effect of debt financing.
   b) Many argue that there is no burden because most of the debt is internal debt.
   c) Persons who buy debt bear a burden in the form of the utility loss they incur in buying the security.
   d) The burden on future generations can be offset by the benefits which come from capital projects.

___ 20. The benefits of debt finance include:
   a) more efficient matching of the temporal stream of the costs and benefits from a capital project.
   b) increased consumption opportunities for the current generation.
   c) better allocation of costs when the population is mobile and the jurisdiction is subnational.
   d) all of the above.

Short Answer Questions: Answer in the space provided.

1. Make a list of five potential projects to be undertaken at the state or local level and for which government borrowing would be an especially attractive means of finance.

2. Go through back issues of local newspapers and try to make a list of three recent projects which local government financed with debt. How were these projects approved? Does debt finance appear to be appropriate for these projects? Why or why not?

Problems: Be sure to show your work.

1. Some economists argue that the level of savings is not sensitive to the interest rate. If savings makes up the supply of loanable funds, how does this alter the analysis of the economic effects of the federal deficit? A graph may help you to compose your answer.

2. If all debt were internal debt, would there be any burden from this debt?

SKETCH ANSWERS TO CHAPTER 12

Issue in Brief:

1. The built-in stabilizers in the budget affect the budget balance in any given year by changing spending for entitlement programs and influencing the amount of taxes colected. In 1998 the U.S. economy was booming at full employment which kept government entitlement spending down and increaased tax collections. The better than anticipated performance of the U.S. economy helped to turn a projected deficit into a surplus!

2. The aging of the population will increase spending for Social Security pensions and government-financed health care programs (Medicare and Medicaid). As the proportion of the population eligible for these programs increases spending will increase rapidly and could result in deficit finace if the Congress does not raise taxes or cut the level of these benefits or limit eligibility.

True/False:

1. T
2. F   They can be regarded as structural.
3. T
4. F   The deficits were not motivated by fiscal policy.
5. F   The target was a reduced deficit by FY95.
6. F   They can contribute to a higher deficit.
7. T
8. T
9. F   A deficit contributes to higher interest rates according to the traditional view.
10. T

11. T
12. T
13. F It would take more than two full years of government spending.
14. T
15. F It involves an outflow of resources.
16. T
17. T
18. F They are more risky.
19. F A higher proportion is external.
20. T
21. T
22. F For example, increased savings by current generations can help offset the burden.
23. T

Multiple Choice:

1.	b	6.	d	11.	c	16.	b
2.	d	7.	b	12.	b	17.	d
3.	b	8.	a	13.	b	18.	d
4.	b	9.	e	14.	e	19.	c
5.	e	10.	b	15.	a	20.	d

Short Answer:

1. Compare your answers with those of your classmates. In general, the projects should be long-term capital projects whose benefits will not begin for several years.

2. Compare your answers with those of your classmates. Be sure to discuss your reasoning. Attaching copies of the newspaper articles may make reviewing your answers easier and provide a reference for future studying.

Problems:

1. The supply of loanable funds is now perfectly inelastic. *Ceteris paribus*, this increases the rise in the interest rate which results from an increase in the demand for loanable funds. This is likely to exacerbate crowding out. On the other hand, a given increase in the supply of loanable funds, such as that hypothesized by the new view, will result in greater downward pressure on the market interest rate. You should be able to draw graphs to convince yourself of these conclusions.

2. From a societal point of view, there is no loss in resources from the repayment of internal debt. However, to the extent that a citizen is not a creditor of the government and does not get benefits from the funded projects, they lose out in paying taxes to retire the debt. An evaluation of the redistributional aspects of debt repayment may lead one to conclude that there is a positive burden even with internal debt.

Chapter Recap: You should now be able to answer the following questions:

1. What are the different types of budget deficits?

2. Describe some of the reasons for budget deficits in the United States.

3. Briefly outline the general history of government budget deficits and debt finance in the United States.

4. What are the economic effects of government budget deficits? Are these effects controversial? How do these effects differ depending on the level of government at which the deficit is incurred?

5. What role does government debt play as a finance tool of government in the United States?

6. Describe the different types of government debt. How do their economic implications differ?

7. What effects do economic fluctuations have on the value of government debt?

8. Describe the unique issues confronted in debt finance by state and local governments.

CHAPTER 13

The Theory of Income Taxation

Chapter Objectives: After reading and working through this chapter, you should understand:

1. The issues involved in defining a personal income tax base.

2. The concept of comprehensive income and how it is measured using the Haig-Simons definition.

3. The economic effects of a tax on labor earnings.

4. The economic effects of a tax on interest income.

5. The notion of tax-base elasticity and its implications for revenue generation.

6. The relationship between income tax rates and tax revenue.

Chapter Summary:

1. Taxes on personal income are the dominant source of general revenue for the federal government in the United States and a major source of revenue for state and local governments. These taxes are relatively new in the United States, only dating back to the early part of the twentieth century. This chapter examines the definition of an appropriate personal income tax base, the economic effects of income taxes, the notion of tax-base elasticity, and the relationship between income tax rates and tax revenue.

2. Preliminary to defining the income tax base, basic decisions must be made regarding the appropriate taxpaying unit and the time period over which income will be measured. Conventionally, these decisions result in the choice of the household as the taxpaying unit and the calendar year as the relevant time period. Under a progressive tax system, both choices can result in distortions due to the change in tax bills that can occur as a result of combining the incomes of household members or by altering the timing of income.

3. *Comprehensive income* is the sum of a person's annual consumption expenditures and the increment in that person's net worth in a given year. Comprehensive income is measured in real terms, includes both realized and unrealized capital gains, and makes no distinctions between sources of income (including business income). It provides a wide-ranging measure of the individual's power to purchase goods and services with the given year. The only allowed deductions would be for the costs of acquiring income. Difficulty in defining legitimate costs of earning income, treating income-in-kind, and measuring unrealized capital gains makes comprehensive income a difficult measure to implement as a personal income tax base. Nevertheless, a comprehensive income tax provides a benchmark for other income taxes in that it would not distort choices in income-producing activities or the pattern of consumption. It also eliminates any need for a separate tax on business or corporate income.

4. Even a comprehensive income tax is likely to distort choices between work and leisure and between consumption and savings or investment. These issues are extremely important, especially since labor income accounts for nearly 80 percent of gross income in the United States, and investment has feedback effects which permeate the economy and have much to do with economic growth.

5. The impact of income taxation on the work-leisure choice cannot be predicted unequivocally. An increase in a tax on labor income decreases the relative price of leisure. Thus, the substitution effect of the tax would increase the consumption of leisure- that is, reduce the amount of work. The same increased tax reduces the net wage and income at all levels of work. The reduction in income reduces the consumption of all normal goods including leisure. Thus, the income effect tends to be favorable to work effort. The relative magnitudes of the income and substitution effects determine the overall effect on the number of hours worked.

6. The impact of taxes on labor income, market wages, net wages, and efficiency depends of the responsiveness of workers to tax-induced wage decreases. The tax introduces a wedge between the gross wage paid by employers and the net wage received by workers, creating distortions which result in excess burden. Even if the uncompensated market supply curve of labor is perfectly inelastic, the excess burden of the tax will not be zero since the compensated labor supply curve, the relevant one for excess burden calculations, will have a positive wage elasticity. However, a perfectly inelastic uncompensated labor supply means that the net wage will fall by the full amount of the tax, indicating that workers bear the full burden of the tax in this circumstance. The situation differs slightly when the uncompensated elasticity of supply of labor exceeds zero. Once again, the excess burden is a function of the substitution effect. *Ceteris paribus*, the excess burden of the tax will be greater than when the supply of labor is perfectly inelastic. Use of the uncompensated labor supply curve underestimates excess burden. When the uncompensated supply curve of

labor is not perfectly inelastic, workers can shift the tax to other groups. In general, empirical analysis estimates the efficiency-loss ratio due to the tax system that prevailed in the 1970s averaged in the range of 5 to 30 percent of revenues collected.

7. A *payroll tax* is essentially a tax on labor income levied on both the employee and the employer. The incidence of the payroll tax is dependent upon the elasticity of the supply of labor. Perfectly inelastic labor supply would result in the full shifting backward to workers of the employer's portion of the tax (independent of the statutory incidence of the tax).

8. Taxation of interest income creates a wedge between the interest received by savers and that paid by borrowers, resulting in excess burden from the tax. Taxation of interest income also results in conflicting income and substitution effects. The substitution effect results in less saving due to the reduced return on net savings. The income effect provides an incentive to reduce the consumption of all normal goods in all time periods, which reduces current consumption and hence increases saving (future consumption is reduced by the tax itself). The actual effect of the tax depends on the relative magnitudes of the income and substitution effects. This is partially dependent upon the magnitude of the interest elasticity of supply of saving, about which there has been much controversy. Many economists believe this magnitude to be near zero, but some recent empirical studies have placed its value much higher. Only when the interest elasticity is zero will the tax be borne exclusively by savers.

9. The *elasticity of the tax base* is the ratio of the percentage change in the tax base attributable to any given percentage change in the tax rate applied to that base. The elasticity may take on either a positive or negative value. If the elasticity is negative, the change in the tax rate and the change in the tax base move in opposite directions. Hence, if the elasticity is less than -1, an increase in the tax rate reduces tax revenue and a decrease in the tax rate increases tax revenue. Tax-base elasticity is determined by the ability to engage in substitute nontaxed activities, the ability to move to a jurisdiction without the tax, and the ability and willingness to engage in other forms of tax avoidance or evasion.

Issue in Brief: The Comeback of Income Tax Reform

Less than ten years after the sweeping Tax Reform Act of 1986, Congress began substantive discussions aimed at another fundamental overhaul of the federal income tax system. Despite reforms, there had continued to be and continues to be deep public discontent with our tax system. This discontent fed through to legislators and 1998 several major tax reform proposals were being discussed in Congress. Though different in substance, these proposals all generally sought to induce Americans to save and invest more of their money through various provisions making all or a part of savings and investment nontaxable. Interestingly, most of the suggested reforms represent ideas that were discussed and rejected during the 1986 debates. Recycled proposals include greatly increased personal exemptions, flat taxes (ranging from 10% to 25% depending on the proposal), consumption taxes, and expanded favorable tax treatment of all forms of savings and investment. Most proposals still retain sacred deductions like the home mortgage deduction and charitable contributions despite their acknowledged distortionary economic effects, providing clear evidence of the importance of issues other than efficiency in making federal tax policy.

Questions for Discussion:

1. Is an income tax that applies a flat tax rate of 17 percent after exempting the first $26,000 of income proportional, progressive, or regressive in its structure?

2. Would any of the tax proposals mentioned seem to move us closer to using Haig-Simons income as our measure of taxable income?

CHAPTER REVIEW QUESTIONS

True/False Questions: If false, explain how to correct the statement to make it true.

1. Taxes on personal income are the dominant source of revenue for the federal government in the United States.

2. In the United States, the taxpaying unit for the personal income tax is the individual.

3. Under a progressive income tax, defining income over an annual time interval may result in individuals with the same income over a ten-year period paying different total amounts of income taxes.

4. Sources of income need not equal uses of income in a given time period.

5. Comprehensive income excludes unrealized capital gains.

6. Taxes represent a use of income.

7. Income-in-kind often results from home production of goods and services.

8. Failure to tax nonpecuniary returns distorts occupational choice.

9. A proportional tax on comprehensive income is non-distortionary.

10. The impact of income taxation on the choice to work can be predicted unequivocally.

11. An income tax increases the opportunity cost of leisure.

12. Use of an uncompensated market labor supply curve underestimates the excess burden of a tax on labor earnings.

13. If the uncompensated market labor supply curve is perfectly inelastic, the excess burden of a tax on labor earnings will be zero.

14. When the uncompensated supply of labor is perfectly inelastic, the incidence of taxes on labor income will be borne entirely by workers.

15. The income effect of a tax on interest income decreases the incentive to save.

16. Analysis suggests that wages are decreased by a tax on interest income.

17. The elasticity of the tax base is always less than or equal to zero.

18. Empirical research suggests that investment demand is more elastic than the supply of savings.

19. The bulk of realized capital gains in the United States comes from the appreciation of real-estate assets.

20. Since the 1970s, the excess burden of the United States income tax system has increased.

21. The income tax can result in significant losses in efficiency in labor markets even though the overall wage elasticity of supply is close to zero.

22. The payroll tax has been the fastest growing tax in the United States in recent years.

23. There is little evidence to suggest that preferential tax treatment of capital gains encourages the formation of new businesses.

24. The general consensus among economists is that both work effort and investment are highly responsive to changes in tax rates.

Multiple Choice Questions: Choose the best answer.

1. The personal income tax became a permanent feature of the federal tax structure in the United States in:
   a) 1789.
   b) 1776.
   c) 1853.
   d) 1927.
   e) 1913.

2. The taxpaying unit for the personal income tax in the United States is:
   a) the household.
   b) the family.
   c) the individual.
   d) the living unit.

3. In an economic sense, income is:
   a) the monetary payments one receives from employers.
   b) the same as wealth.
   c) a measure of a person's power to purchase goods and services in a given year.
   d) only defined in terms of its uses.
   e) all of the above.

4. The value of a person's assets held at any point in time less the value of a person's liabilities is called:
   a) income.
   b) net worth.
   c) capital gain.
   d) nonpecuniary wealth.

5. Which of the following is a source of income?
   a) Social Security pensions.
   b) gifts from one's parents.
   c) the gain in value of IBM stock which is not sold.
   d) salary from a job as a teacher.
   e) all of the above.

6. According to the Haig-Simons definition of income, which of the following qualifies as consumption?
   a) a donation to Northern Illinois University.
   b) a cash gift to your parents.
   c) purchase of an automobile.
   d) all of the above.

7. Increases in the value of assets in a given year that accrue on assets that are not sold for cash or exchanged for other assets are called:
   a) nonpecuniary income.
   b) nonmarket transfers.
   c) realized capital gains.
   d) unrealized capital gains.

8. Which of the following is true?
   a) Sources of income is greater than uses of income.
   b) Uses of income is greater than sources of income.
   c) Sources of income equals uses of income.
   d) none of the above.

9. Which of the following makes measurement of Haig-Simons income difficult?
   a) calculation of the expenses of earning income.
   b) measurement of capital gains.
   c) valuation of nonpecuniary income.
   d) treatment of income-in-kind.
   e) all of the above.

10. Income in the form of goods and services:
    a) is never taxable.
    b) is always taxable.
    c) decreases a consumer's purchasing power.
    d) is income-in-kind.

11. A general proportional tax on comprehensive income:
    a) distorts the ratio of the price of labor to the price of capital.
    b) distorts the relative prices of consumption goods.
    c) treats sources of income unevenly.
    d) distorts choices involving the allocation of income between consumption and saving.

12. With convex indifference curves, the substitution effect of a tax on labor income:
    a) increases hours worked.
    b) decreases hours worked.
    c) has no effect on hours worked.
    d) affects hours worked ambiguously.

13. With perfectly inelastic uncompensated labor supply:
    a) there is no excess burden from a tax on labor income.
    b) employers bear the entire burden of a tax on labor income.
    c) workers bear the entire burden of a tax on labor income.
    d) employers and workers share the burden of a tax on labor income.

14. The marginal rate of time preference is:
    a) the absolute value of the slope of an indifference curve for present and future consumption.
    b) generally presumed to exceed one for most persons.
    c) is a measure of the willingness of savers to forego current consumption in exchange for future consumption.
    d) all of the above.

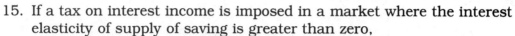

15. If a tax on interest income is imposed in a market where the interest elasticity of supply of saving is greater than zero,
    a) there will be no excess burden form the tax.
    b) the net interest rate will increase.
    c) the tax will be borne exclusively by savers.
    d) the tax can be shifted from savers to borrowers.

16. Relative to a lump-sum tax, a tax on interest income will likely result in:
    a) decreased investment.
    b) lower wages.
    c) a lower ratio of capital to labor.
    d) reduced capital stock growth.
    e) all of the above.

17. A flat-rate tax on labor income will
    a. always reduce hours worked per year.
    b. always increase hours worked per year.
    c. either increase or decrease hours worked per year.
    d. never have any effect on the amount of leisure hours per year.

18. A tax on interest income
    a. cause the gross interest rate paid by investors to exceed the net interest rate received by savers.
    b. will always reduce saving.
    c. will always increase saving.
    d. is equivalent to a lump-sum tax.

19. Using a regular labor supply curve instead of a compensated supply curve to calculate the excess burden of a tax on labor income will
    a. result in an accurate estimate of the excess burden.
    b. will overestimate the excess burden.
    c. will understimate the excess burden.
    d. will accurately estimate the excess burden only if the market supply of labor is perfectly inelastic.

20. Income taxes can affect labor supply by influencing:
    a) intensity of work.
    b) investment in human capital.
    c) retirement decisions.
    d) choice of occupation.
    e) all of the above.

Short Answer Questions: Answer in the space provided.

1. Think of two jobs, one which you might want to hold and one that you would not. Which job pays a higher wage? Identify nonpecuniary returns (these may be negative) which contribute to the wage differential between the two jobs.

2. Make a list of five different types of income-in-kind. Are any of the forms easily taxable? How could one go about measuring the value of this in-kind income?

Problems: Be sure to show your work.

1. You are offered the following information regarding the finances of an individual during a given year:

Donations to charity:	7,500.00
Purchases of goods and services:	18,000.00
Purchase of saving certificate:	6,000.00
Sales taxes paid:	1,200.00
Receipts from the sale of stock valued at $1,000 as of beginning of year:	1,500.00
Costs of purchasing job supplies:	400.00

   What is this person's Haig-Simons income?

2. Look at Figure 13.6 in your textbook. Assume that the supply of savings curve in the figure is uncompensated and that income effects are not negligible. Draw a figure which would correctly analyze the excess burden of this tax.

SKETCH ANSWERS TO CHAPTER 13

Issue in Brief:

1. The structure is progressive due to the exemption. Average effective tax rates increase with income.

2. Only those that reduce deductions. Otherwise, the reform efforts, like most in the past, did not seem to be aimed at broadening the income sources subject to taxation.

True/False:

1. T
2. F   The unit is the household.
3. T
4. F   They must be equal.
5. F   Unrealized capital gains are included.
6. T
7. T
8. T
9. F   For example, it distorts the work-leisure choice.
10. F   It cannot be predicted unequivocally.
11. F   The opportunity cost is decreased.
12. T
13. F   Excess burden will not be zero.
14. T
15. F   Savings increases.
16. T
17. F   It may be positive.
18. T
19. T
20. F   Excess burden has declined due to lower tax rates.
21. T
22. T
23. T
24. F   Consensus is that they are highly unresponsive.

Multiple Choice:

1.	e	6.	d	11.	d	16.	e
2.	a	7.	d	12.	b	17.	c
3.	c	8.	c	13.	c	18.	a
4.	b	9.	e	14.	d	19.	c
5.	e	10.	d	15.	d	20.	e

Short Answer:

1. Compare your answers with those of your classmates.

2. Compare your answers with those of your classmates. Many of the issues here are similar to those encountered in enumerating and evaluating costs and benefits during cost-benefit analysis.

Problems:

1. $32,800 including a realized capital gain of $500 and a reduction in income due to $400 in job-related expenses.

2. Use of the uncompensated supply curve would cause excess burden to be underestimated. Thus, a compensated supply curve must be used. The analysis proceeds in exactly the same fashion as illustrated in Figure 13.4 in your text.

Chapter Recap: You should now be able to answer the following questions:

1. What kinds of issues are faced in defining the personal income tax base? What about the choice of the taxpaying unit?

2. What is comprehensive income? How is it measured using the Haig-Simons definition?

3. Describe the economic effects of a tax on labor earnings. A graph may help elucidate your answer.

4. Describe the economic effects of a tax on interest income. A graph may help elucidate your answer.

CHAPTER 14

Taxation of Personal Income in the United States

Chapter Objectives: After reading and working through this chapter, you should understand:

1. The definition of taxable income in the United States.

2. The rate structure of the personal income tax in the United States.

3. The notion of tax preferences and their specific form in the federal income tax.

4. The efficiency losses from tax preferences.

5. The financial advantages of tax deferral.

6. Current general issues in U.S. tax policy, including the economic effects of income taxation.

Chapter Summary:

1. This chapter describes the personal income tax law in the United States and discusses economic issues in tax policy as they relate to the federal personal income tax.

2. *Taxable income* is the portion of income received by individuals that is subject to the personal income tax. Taxable income in the United States is considerably less broad than Haig-Simons income and thus is smaller in magnitude. *Gross income* is all income received during the year from taxable sources. This includes wages and salaries, interest from taxable sources, dividends, rental income, profits from business activity, and realized capital gains. Certain sources of income are not taxed, creating a distortion. Among these are most in-kind income and unrealized capital gains. *Adjusted gross income* is gross income minus allowable adjustments such as reimbursed employee business expenses and contributions by the individual to special retirement plans. Once adjusted gross income is computed, personal exemptions and deductions are subtracted from it to obtain taxable income. In general, one personal exemption is allowed for each dependent (including

the taxpayer) claimed on the tax return. For most taxpayers in 1998, the personal exemption was $2700 for each dependent claimed and could only be claimed on one tax return for each individual. Deductions may either be taken in the form of a lump-sum standard deduction or through itemizing deductions for expenses which can be legally subtracted in the computation of taxable income. Both the personal exemption and standard deduction are now indexed for inflation.

3. The federal income tax now has five brackets, with a maximum marginal tax rate of 39.6 percent. Different tax rates apply to different taxpayers depending on their filing status (for example, single, married filing jointly, married filing separately). Phaseout is also dependent upon the number of exemptions claimed.

4. The personal exemptions and standard deduction imply that a substantial portion of the income of low-income taxpayers is nontaxable. In addition, low-income taxpayers with dependent children are eligible for a special payment from the government if they work. The *earned income tax credit* is a refundable credit which reduces the taxes owed by workers by an amount equal to a certain percentage of wage and salary income for those eligible. The earned income tax credit provides a tax refund for those not owing any tax! The credit rises with wage and salary income at first and is eventually phased out as income increases.

5. *Effective tax rates* are actual taxes paid divided by the taxable base. The taxable base here is a measure of gross income. Estimates suggest progressiveness in the effective tax rates of the federal personal income tax.

6. *Tax preferences* are exclusions, exemptions, and deductions from the tax base. They subsidize certain economic activities and thus create behavioral distortions which result in excess burden. Tax preferences are justified on the basis of the administrative difficulty in taxing certain activities, improving equity, or a desire to encourage certain private expenditures that generate external benefits. Tax preferences in the United States include personal exemptions, exclusion of income-in-kind, exclusion of most transfer income, exclusion of unrealized capital gains, exclusion of interest income from state and local bonds, as well as tax deductions for those who itemize. Itemized deductions include home mortgage interest, catastrophic medical expenses, and state and local property and income taxes.

7. Deferral of taxable income postpones tax liability. The ability to accrue interest tax free, and to protect the principal, as the tax burden is postponed results in a significant financial advantage to tax deferral.

8. The dollar value of tax credits is the same in every tax bracket. A one dollar tax credit reduces the taxpayer's tax liability by one dollar. On the other hand, a tax deduction reduces the taxpayer's taxable income. Hence, a one dollar tax deduction will have a differing value depending on the taxpayer's tax bracket. The higher the tax bracket, the more valuable the deduction.

9. Any reduction in marginal tax rates for most taxpayers means that the excess burden from tax preferences will be reduced. Relative prices are less distorted by the lower subsidies present in tax preferences which are based on lower marginal tax rates.

10. *Tax expenditures* are losses in tax revenues attributable to tax preferences. The Congressional Budget Reform Act of 1974 requires OMB to compute tax expenditures annually and to submit them as part of the president's budget message to Congress.

11. Major issues in income tax policy in the United States have included the treatment of inflation, especially in terms of tax brackets, interest income, and capital gains; as well as the issue of appropriate definition of a tax structure that does not discriminate by type of household. Inflation can result in increased effective tax rates if tax brackets are not adjusted, nominal interest is taxed rather than real returns, and nominal capital gains are not adjusted for inflation. The first problem has been addressed through recent indexing, but the last two problems remain. There is still some discrimination in the rate structure against married couples with similar incomes who file jointly. This discrimination is known as the marriage tax and provides some disincentive to marriage.

Issue in Brief: Taxation of Fringe Benefits

Despite many reform efforts, one of the areas of continuing inconsistent and inefficient tax treatment in the present Internal Revenue Code is in the area of in-kind benefits (i.e., fringe benefits). One possible solution was framed in a law journal article written shortly after the Tax Reform Act of 1986 failed to make much progress in this area of the tax code. In that article, my coauthor and I argued that in general in-kind benefits which trigger an allowable tax deduction for the employer should be presumed to generate an economic benefit and therefore taxable income to the employee. Exceptions to this rule would only apply to fringe benefits of negligible value, modest employee discounts (using the existing "twenty percent rule" as guidance), benefits which would generate a valid employee expense tax deduction for the employee if paid directly by the employee instead, and those benefits which should be excluded from taxation on the basis of overriding social interest (e.g., life insurance proceeds paid as a death benefit to survivors). For further information, see Michael T. Peddle and Scott Sandstrom, "Developing a Logical Framework Regarding the Tax Treatment of Employee Benefits," *Journal of Contemporary Law*, 1987, pp. 249-276.

Questions for Discussion:

1. What would be some of the fringe benefits that would be taxable under this proposal?

2. What would be some examples of negligible value fringes?

CHAPTER REVIEW QUESTIONS

True/False Questions: If false, explain how to correct the statement to make it true.

____ 1. United States taxpayers can affect their personal income tax bills by controlling the sources and uses of their income.

____ 2. Taxable income exceeds adjusted gross income.

____ 3. Some taxpayers receive no personal exemption. *(if claimed as a dependent by someone else)*

____ 4. There is a single tax rate structure for all taxpayers filing United States personal income tax forms.

____ 5. A substantial portion of the income of low-income taxpayers is nontaxable.

____ 6. Effective tax rates exceed statutory tax rates.

____ 7. Tax preferences distort the relative prices of preferred items and activities.

____ 8. The value of a tax preference generally varies with the taxpayer's tax bracket.

____ 9. A reduction in the marginal tax rates significantly increases the excess burden resulting from those tax preferences that remain in the tax code.

____ 10. The United States federal tax code treats transfer income consistently.

____ 11. Only realized capital gains are included in taxable income.

____ 12. Under current income tax rules, capital gains are not taxed at death.

____ 13. The financial advantage to postponing tax liability can be enormous.

____ 14. State and local sales taxes are an allowable itemized deduction.

____ 15. Studies find that charitable giving is highly responsive to tax deductibility.

____ 16. A minimum tax is levied on taxapayers who make extensive use of tax preferences.

____ 17. Those who favor an increase in the progressivity of the federal tax rate structure generally favor tax deductions over tax credits.

18. Elimination of tax preferences narrows the tax base.

19. Inflation creates serious problems in accurately measuring interest income and capital gains.

20. Inflation causes nominal capital income to grow less rapidly than labor income.

21. The standard deduction for married couples is less than the sum of that for two single people.

22. The joint rate schedule provides benefits to taxpayers only to the extent to which the income of the two spouses is equal.

Multiple Choice: Choose the best answer.

1. Taxable income in the United States is:
   a) considerably less than Haig-Simons income.
   b) less than one-half of personal income.
   c) the portion of income received by individuals which is subject to the personal income tax.
   d) all of the above.

2. Which of the following is not included in gross income?
   a) wages and salaries.
   b) imputed rental income.
   c) realized capital gains.
   d) net gambling gains.
   e) none of the above.

3. A ranking of income measures from largest to smallest would be:
   a) comprehensive income, taxable income, adjusted gross income, personal income.
   b) comprehensive income, gross income, adjusted gross income, taxable income.
   c) gross income, comprehensive income, adjusted gross income, taxable income.
   d) comprehensive income, adjusted gross income, gross income, personal income.

4. Which of the following is an allowable adjustment to gross income?
   a) alimony paid.
   b) reimbursed employee business expenses.
   c) penalties for early withdrawal of savings.
   d) contributions to special retirement plans.
   e) all of the above.

5. A range of income subject to a given marginal tax rate is a:
   a) tax bracket.
   b) tax exemption.
   c) tax credit.
   d) defined tax program.

6. The very highest income taxpayers in the United States are subject to a marginal tax rate of:
   a) 15 percent.
   b) 28 percent.
   c) 31 percent.
   d) 39.6 percent.
   e) 46 percent.

7. Tax expenditures are
   a) expenditures made to collect taxes.
   b) losses in revenue due to tax preferences.
   c) less than one percent of tax revenue.
   d) both (b) and (c).

8. Actual taxes paid divided by the taxable base defines the:
   a) net tax rate.
   b) gross tax rate.
   c) effective tax rate.
   d) tax liability.
   e) none of the above.

9. Which of the following offers a justification for tax preferences?
   a) administrative difficulty in taxing certain activities.
   b) improving equity.
   c) encouraging private expenditures that generate external benefits.
   d) all of the above.

10. Tax preferences generally:
   a) decrease efficiency by encouraging more than the efficient amount of an activity to be undertaken.
   b) decrease efficiency by encouraging less than the efficient amount of an activity to be undertaken.
   c) create no economic distortions.
   d) none of the above.

11. Which of the following is excluded from income under the U.S. income tax?
   a) income from the rental of apartments.
   b) employer-provided health insurance.
   c) unemployment compensation.
   d) realized capital gains.

12. Scholarships and fellowships:
    a) are excluded from income for all students.
    b) are excluded from income for degree candidates only.
    c) are excluded only to the extent to which they do not exceed tuition
       and other course-related expenses.
    d) b and c only.
    e) none of the above.

13. Which of the following is not an allowable itemized deduction?
    a) unreimbursed medical expenses in excess of 7.5 percent of
       adjusted gross income.
    b) interest on a $2 million home mortgage.
    c) local property taxes.
    d) charitable contributions.

14. The value of a tax deduction:
    a) is greater for taxpayers in higher marginal tax brackets.
    b) is lower for taxpayers in higher marginal tax brackets.
    c) does not vary by tax bracket.
    d) decreases as a tax system becomes more progressive.

15. The value of a tax credit:
    a) is greater for taxpayers in higher marginal tax brackets.
    b) is lower for taxpayers in higher marginal tax brackets.
    c) does not vary by tax bracket.
    d) decreases as a tax system becomes more progressive.

16. Any reduction in marginal tax rates for most taxpayers means that:
    a) the excess burden from tax preferences will be increased.
    b) the excess burden from tax preferences will be reduced.
    c) the tax base will be narrowed.
    d) the value of tax preferences will be increased.
    e) a and d only.

17. Losses in revenues attributable to tax preferences are called:
    a) tax distortions.
    b) excess burden.
    c) tax expenditures.
    d) tax deductions.

18. Which of the following is the largest tax expenditure in the United
    States individual income tax?
    a) deductibility of mortgage interest on owner-occupied housing.
    b) net exclusion from income of pension contributions and earnings.
    c) exclusion of Social Security benefits.
    d) deductibility of charitable contributions.

19. Inflation creates which of the following problems?
    a) bracket creep.
    b) difficulty in measuring interest income.
    c) overstating interest deductions.
    d) reduced capital mobility.
    e) all of the above.

20. The average tax rate for two equal-income married taxpayers is:
    a) higher than the corresponding rate for two spouses with unequal incomes.
    b) lower than the corresponding rate for two spouses with equal incomes.
    c) higher than the corresponding rate for two single taxpayers with the same incomes.
    d) higher than the corresponding rate for a single taxpayer with an income equal to the total income of the two spouses.

Short Answer Questions: Answer in the space provided.

1. List six tax preferences under the present federal income tax. What is the basis for each of these preferences? In what way does each of these preferences affect relative prices?

2. Based upon your reading and your knowledge of the personal income tax in the United States, make two reform suggestions designed to improve this tax system. On what basis should your reforms be adopted?

Problems: Be sure to show your work.

1. Assume that an individual in the 15 percent marginal tax bracket puts $5000 into a Keogh retirement plan. The account earns 12 percent per year. If the money is to be held for ten years, calculate the benefit of tax deferral. If the individual were in the 28 percent tax bracket instead, would the benefit by greater or lesser than this calculated benefit?

2. A taxpayer has wage and salary income of $20,000, receives a $4000 health insurance policy which is fully paid by her employer, has imputed rent from her house of $8400 annually, pays $800 per year in home mortgage interest, donates $2000 per year to the American Heart Association, received alimony payments of $3000, incurred penalties for the early withdrawal of savings amounting to $2700, and is single, not qualifying to itemize deductions. What is the taxpayer's gross income? Her adjusted gross income? Her taxable income (using the 1988 laws outlined in your textbook)?

SKETCH ANSWERS TO CHAPTER 14

Issue in Brief:

1. e.g., employer-paid life insurance, group legal services, dependent care assistance (above the benefit in the existing tax credit), free tuition for dependent's of college professors (a modest discount would still be allowed).

2. e.g., typing of an occasional personal letter by a secretary, notary public services, limited personal use of copying machine, occasional company picnics or parties, on-premises coffee and doughnuts, cab fare when occasionally working late.

True/False:

1. T
2. F   AGI is larger.
3. T
4. F   The structure varies by filing status.
5. T
6. F   Statutory rates are always higher.
7. T
8. T
9. F   It will reduce excess burden.
10. F   Transfers are treated inconsistently.
11. T
12. T
13. T
14. F   These taxes are not deductible.
15. T
16. T
17. F   They favor tax credits over tax deductions.
18. F   It widens the gap.
19. T
20. F   Capital income grows more rapidly.
21. T
22. F   Benefits occur only to the extent that one spouse has a significantly higher income than the other.

Multiple Choice:

1. d	6. d	11. b	16. b
2. b	7. b	12. d	17. c
3. b	8. c	13. b	18. b
4. e	9. d	14. a	19. e
5. a	10. a	15. c	20. c

Short Answer:

1. Compare your answers with those of your classmates. Justifications for tax preferences are outlined in your text. Tax preferred activities have their relative prices reduced.

2. Compare your answers with those of your classmates. Recall the criteria for judging tax systems and try to be specific about applying these criteria to your reform proposals.

Problems:

1. Net income if nontaxable is $8949.85. Net income if taxable is $6975.48. Thus, there is a substantial subsidy from tax deferral. This subsidy would be greater with a higher marginal tax rate.

2. Gross income is $23,000. Adjusted gross income is $20,300. Taxable income is $15,300 using a standard deduction of $3000 and a personal exemption of $2000.

Chapter Recap: You should now be able to answer the following questions:

1. How is taxable income defined in the United States federal personal income tax?

2. Describe the rate structure of the personal income tax in the United States.

3. What are tax preferences? What form do they take in the federal income tax?

4. Carefully describe the efficiency losses from tax preferences. A graph may help to elucidate your answer.

5. What are the financial advantages of tax deferral? Be precise.

6. What are some of the major issues faced in current United States' income tax policy? As part of your answer, be sure to discuss the economic effects of income taxation.

CHAPTER 15

Taxation of Corporate Income

Chapter Objectives: After reading and working through this chapter, you should understand:

1. The general issues involved in the taxation of business income.

2. The issues and problems involved in the separate taxation of corporate income.

3. The tax base of the corporation income tax in the United States.

4. The tax rate structure of the corporation income tax in the United States.

5. The economic effects of a tax on corporate profits.

6. The economic incidence and effects of the corporation income tax.

Chapter Summary:

1. This chapter discusses the issues involved in the taxation of corporations and business income in general. The structure and economic effects of the United States corporate income tax are also discussed.

2. In the United States, the corporate form of business is treated as a separate and distinct taxpaying entity. The owners of a corporation are its shareholders, who are protected by the provision of limited liability. Under a comprehensive personal income tax, separate taxation of corporate income would not be necessary because corporate income would be allocated to shareholders on a pro rata basis. Under our current tax system, a corporate income tax is often justified as a tax on the special privileges which accrue from the corporate form of business and because tax preferences exclude unrealized capital gains from the personal income tax base. In addition, the absence of a separate tax on corporate income would allow undistributed corporate profits to escape taxation and would thus create incentives to plow profits back into the business rather than using them to pay dividends. Dividends are taxed by both the corporate and the personal income taxes.

3. The present United States tax system creates distortions in corporate financing, biasing the corporation toward the use of debt finance. Leveraged buyouts have been a manifestation of this bias. The tax system allows interest costs on external debts to be deducted, but allows no such deductions for equity finance or the use of undistributed corporate profits. Dividends are not tax deductible. Numerous firms have replaced equity with debt. Recent reform proposals have attempted to eliminate this distortion, but have not yet been put into place.

4. The tax base on which the corporate income tax is levied comprises total corporate profits. The tax base allows no deductions for the opportunity cost of capital the firm supplies itself and taxes normal profits. This contributes to the bias toward debt finance and results in economic distortions. Further distortions are created through the application of arbitrary depreciation rules which diverge significantly from the *economic depreciation* of assets, that is the value of durable physical capital used up in the productive process. *Accelerated depreciation* allows a firm to deduct more than the actual economic depreciation from its income each year. This results in windfall gains in the form of tax reductions for the firm. The Tax Reform Act of 1986 significantly reduced the availability and value of accelerated depreciation. On the other side of the tax equation, depreciation and inventory valuations based upon historic cost have increased the effective taxes paid by corporations through understatement of capital consumption and inventory costs.

5. Despite the corporate income tax's nominal progressivity, the tax is basically a flat-rate tax for large corporations. It carries a 35 percent marginal tax rate, since all lower tax brackets are phased out for corporations with annual incomes greater than $335,000. Through reform of accelerated depreciation and the elimination of the investment tax credit, the Tax Reform Act of 1986 increased the effective corporate tax rate, although the statutory rates fell. The appropriate tax burden for corporations is a highly charged political issue. Currently, the effective marginal tax rate on corporate income is higher than that on noncorporate business income.

6. There is great controversy about the short-run impact of the corporate income tax. If firms are profit maximizers and operate in competitive markets, economic theory says that the tax cannot be shifted in the form of higher consumer prices. However, relaxing these assumptions opens the possibility of shifting the tax. Evidence on the short-run impact of the tax on prices is conflicting and varied. Unfortunately, the question of short-run shifting of the tax is of crucial importance in determining the ultimate incidence and excess burden of the tax. This hinges on the impact that the tax has in the short run on the return to capital invested in the corporate sector.

7. Harberger's model of the long-run impact of the corporate income tax assumes that the tax is not shifted in the short run. His model concludes that under these circumstances, in perfectly competitive markets where the corporate income tax is the only tax levied, the burden of the tax will be borne by *all* owners of capital, and that the tax decreases the return to investment earned throughout the economy. The discriminatory treatment of corporate investment distorts the pattern of investment in the economy, resulting in excess burden. This burden has been empirically estimated to be very high. The burden increases with increased interest elasticity of saving. Harberger's model suggests a progressive tax burden.

8. The tax-induced flow of investment caused by the corporate income tax can affect output prices and wages in the long run. In general, we would expect some increase in the price of corporate goods relative to noncorporate goods. The tax-induced decline in capital formation reduces wages across the economy, shifting a portion of the corporate income tax to workers. The actual incidence of the corporate income tax remains unresolved.

Issue in Brief: Why Tax Corporations?

Taxes are paid by people not by organizations. A corporation is an organization that is given its own legal identity under law that allow it to enter into contracts, own property, a pay taxes as *if* it were a person. But a corporation is not really a person. It is a business entity owned entirely by its shareholders. In many ways the issues regarding business taxation are obscured by a separate tax on corporations. The corporation income tax could be abolished and annual corporate income for each corporation could be allocated to individuals based on their ownership of shares of the total corporate stock outstanding. Each person would get an annual statement of their share of total corporate income which they would then declare as personal income when they file their personal income tax return.

Questions for Discussion:

1. Suppose you own 100 shares of the Ford Corporation. If Ford's total income this year is $1 million, and there are one million shares outstanding, then what is your share of the corporation income?

2. How would treating corporate income as personal income make it the distinction between retained earnings and dividends irrelevant for tax purposes?

CHAPTER REVIEW QUESTIONS

True/False Questions: If false, explain how to correct the statement to make it true.

_T_ 1. Stockholders have limited liability for the debts of a corporation.

_F_ 2. Separate taxation of corporate income is needed in the presence of a comprehensive personal income tax.

_T_ 3. Dividends are doubly taxed under the current United States tax system.

_F_ 4. Undistributed corporate profits are not taxed by the corporate income tax.

_T_ 5. In recent years, corporate finance has been biased in favor of equity finance.

_T_ 6. The corporate income tax only taxes economic profits.

_T_ 7. The useful lives of assets, as defined by Internal Revenue Service guidelines, do not always coincide with the actual useful economic lives of the assets.

_T_ 8. In general, assuming a flat-rate tax, the firm's after-tax income in any given year is greater the more quickly it can depreciate its capital expenditures and the greater the proportion of the expenditures it can write off in earlier years of use.

_T_ 9. The Tax Reform Act of 1986 substantially decelerated the recovery periods for most assets.

_T_ 10. Inflation increases the effective rate of taxation on real economic profits.

_F_ 11. The effective marginal tax rate on corporate income is lower than that on business income earned in the noncorporate sector.

_T_ 12. As a result of the Tax Reform Act of 1986, effective marginal tax rates on investment in equipment have risen more sharply than the effective tax rates on structures.

_T_ 13. According to economic theory, a tax on economic profits can be shifted in the short run.

_F_ 14. The corporate income tax in the United States allows firms to deduct the opportunity cost of owner-supplied funds for investment.

___ T 15. According to the Harberger model, the long-run impact of the corporate income tax is borne by all owners of capital across the economy.

___ T 16. Before-tax returns to investment are equal in the corporate and noncorporate sectors of Harberger's model after the tax is introduced and long-run equilibrium is established.

___ F 17. There is no excess burden associated with the corporate income tax.

___ T 18. The cost of financial resources would be deductible under a corporate cash-flow tax.

___ T 19. A corporate cash-flow tax will not distort the pattern of investment between corporate and noncorporate assets.

___ T 20. Introduction of a corporate cash-flow tax may very well be revenue neutral.

___ T 21. *Ceteris paribus*, a multinational firm would prefer to do its borrowing in high-tax jurisdictions.

Multiple Choice Questions: Choose the best answer.

___ D 1. Corporate earnings retained by the corporation to finance expenses are called:
   a) normal profits.
   b) economic profits.
   c) leveraged profits.
   d) undistributed corporate profits.
   e) none of the above.

___ C 2. Under prevailing tax law, by retaining earnings to finance expansion instead of paying the earnings out as dividends and using external funds for expansion, the corporation's net taxable income:
   a) is unaffected.
   b) increases, as does its tax bill.
   c) decreases, as does its tax bill.
   d) decreases, but its tax bill increases.

___ C 3. Under comprehensive personal income taxation,
   a) corporate dividends are double taxed.
   b) a separate corporate income tax would still be necessary.
   c) corporate profits would be distributed to shareholders on a pro rata basis.
   d) all of the above.

4. In recent years,
    a) corporate finance has been biased in favor of equity finance.
    b) revenue collected from the corporate income tax has declined.
    c) corporate finance has been biased in favor of debt finance.
    d) income after tax in leveraged corporations has been lower than that in all-equity corporations.
    e) b and d only.

5. The tax base of the corporate income tax in the United States is:
    a) normal profit only.
    b) economic profit only.
    c) the difference between normal and economic profit.
    d) total corporate profits.

6. The value of the durable physical capital used up in the productive process is called:
    a) the wear value.
    b) accounting depreciation.
    c) economic depreciation.
    d) physical consumption allowance.

7. Which of the following offers the greatest tax advantage to the firm?
    a) accelerated depreciation.
    b) expensing of a capital asset.
    c) straight-line depreciation.
    d) sum-of-the-year's digits depreciation.

8. In the presence of inflation, the use of historic cost as the basis for depreciation calculations:
    a) artificially decreases the firm's income tax bill.
    b) results in an understatement of a firm's profits.
    c) results in an overstatement of a firm's profits.
    d) is convenient and has no effect on the tax bill of the firm in the long run.

9. The Tax Reform Act of 1986:
    a) increased both the statutory and effective marginal tax rates on corporate income.
    b) decreased the statutory but increased the effective marginal tax rates on corporate income.
    c) increased the statutory but increased the effective marginal tax rates on corporate income.
    d) decreased both the statutory and the effective marginal tax rates on corporate income.

10. Which of the following statements about the Tax Reform Act of 1986 is false?
    a) the act evened out tax rates on alternative types of investment.
    b) the act was designed to reduce the taxes paid by corporations.
    c) the act reduced the value of mortgage interest deductions and property tax deductions to homeowners.
    d) the act increased effective tax rates on equipment.

11. Which of the following is estimated to face the highest marginal effective tax rate?
    a) corporate sector investment.
    b) noncorporate sector investment.
    c) investment in owner-occupied housing.
    d) all of the above investments face the same effective tax rate.

12. A tax on economic profits:
    a) only collects revenues in the long run in a competitive industry.
    b) can be shifted in the short run.
    c) affects a firm's marginal costs.
    d) is borne in the short run by the owners of the firm.

13. Forward shifting of the corporation income tax would be evidenced by:
    a) higher consumer prices.
    b) lower consumer prices.
    c) higher wages.
    d) lower wages.

14. The Harberger model of the long-run effects of the corporation income tax assumes that:
    a) the corporate income tax is the only tax being used.
    b) perfect competition prevails in all markets.
    c) the total supply of funds for investment each year is fixed.
    d) the supply of inputs is fixed.
    e) all of the above.

15. The Harberger model concludes that:
    a) the corporate income tax is discriminatory.
    b) the corporate income tax cannot be shifted in the short run.
    c) the burden of the corporate income tax will be borne by the owners of corporations in the long run.
    d) that the supply of funds to the noncorporate sector would increase with a corporate income tax.
    e) all of the above.

16. In the long run, after introduction of a corporate income tax, Harberger's model argues that equilibrium will be such that:
    a) the gross return to corporate investment is less than the net return to corporate investment.
    b) the gross return to noncorporate investment is greater than the gross return to corporate investment.
    c) the net return to noncorporate investment is equated with the net return to corporate investment.
    d) the net return to noncorporate investment is greater than the net return to corporate investment.

17. The excess burden of the corporate income tax:
    a) has been found to be negligible.
    b) is greatest when the interest elasticity of saving is zero.
    c) is a result of the combined distortion in the pattern of investment and a reduction in total investment.
    d) all of the above.

18. Harberger's general conclusion about the long-run burden of the corporate income tax implies that the burden is distributed:
    a) in a progressive manner with respect to income.
    b) in a proportional manner with respect to income.
    c) less progressively than it would be if the tax were shifted in the short run.
    d) in a regressive manner with respect to income.

19. The shifting of the corporate income tax to workers stems from:
    a) the higher wages workers receive.
    b) a tax-induced decline in capital formation.
    c) a tax-induced increase in capital formation.
    d) the higher consumer prices which result.

20. A corporate cash-flow tax would not:
    a) eliminate depreciation of capital acquired by corporations.
    b) distort investment decisions.
    c) eliminate the bias toward debt financing.
    d) increase any firms' taxes.
    e) none of the above.

Short Answer Questions: Answer in the space provided.

1. Based upon your reading and other knowledge, should the United States' corporate income tax be abolished? Why or why not?

2. Should a corporate cash-flow tax be implemented in the United States? Why or why not?

Problems: Be sure to show your work.

1. In a given year, Corporation A has operating income of $275,000. It has interest expenses on its debt amounting to $75,000 and pays out $80,000 in dividends on its stock. Corporation B also has operating income of $275,000. It pays $100,000 in dividends on its stock. It uses $200,000 from its retained earnings to finance a major project. Corporation B could have earned an annual return of 8 percent had the funds remained in retained earnings.

   a) What is Corporation A's taxable income? How much will it owe in corporate income tax?

   b) What is Corporation B's taxable income? How much will it owe in corporate income tax?

   c) Discuss any economic distortions illustrated by this example.

2. Draw a graph of the tax rate structure of the corporate income tax in the United States.

SKETCH ANSWERS TO CHAPTER 15

Issue in Brief:

1. Your share of the corporate ownership is 1/10,000. Your share of the corporate income is therefore $100.

2. Currently only dividends are taxable as personal inceme. Under abolition of the corporation income tax it would make no difference how the corporation handled its earnings, it would be taxed as personal income whether directly paid out or retained therefore contributing to increase in the capital value of the corporation.

True/False:

1. T
2. F   A separate corporate tax would be unnecessary.
3. T
4. F   Undistributed corporate profits are taxed as part of the corporate income tax.
5. F   Bias has been in favor of debt finance.
6. F   Both economic and normal profits are taxed.
7. T
8. T
9. T
10. T

11. F   The effective tax rate on corporate income is higher.
12. T
13. F   The theory of the profit-maximizing firm suggests that the tax cannot be shifted in the short run.
14. F   No such deduction is allowed.
15. T
16. F   After-tax returns are equated.
17. F   The tax distorts the pattern of investment in the economy.
18. F   It is not deductible.
19. T
20. T
21. T

Multiple Choice:

1.	d	6.	c	11.	a	16.	c
2.	b	7.	b	12.	d	17.	c
3.	c	8.	c	13.	a	18.	a
4.	c	9.	b	14.	e	19.	b
5.	d	10.	b	15.	d	20.	b

Short Answer:

1. Compare your answer with those of your classmates. You should consider issues such as double taxation of dividends, the rationale for a separate corporate tax, and the necessity for any reform proposal to replace any lost revenue.

2. Compare your answer with those of your classmates. Be sure to explicitly note your normative judgements and evaluative criteria.

Problems:

1.
   a) Taxable income is $200,000. Corporate income tax owed is $56,250.

   b) Taxable income is $275,000. Corporate income tax owed is $81,750.

   c) This problem illustrates the tax advantage of, and thus the distortionary incentive to use, debt finance.

2. See Figure 14.1 as an example. The graph should show four brackets due to the phaseout of the lower brackets above $335,000 in corporate income.

Chapter Recap: You should now be able to answer the following questions:

1. Carefully discuss the general issues involved in the taxation of business income.

2. Discuss the issues and problems associated with the separate taxation of corporate income.

3. What is the tax base for the corporate income tax in the United States?

4. Describe the tax rate structure of the corporate income tax in the United States.

5. What are the economic effects of a tax on corporate profits? Graphs may help to elucidate your answer.

6. Describe the economic effects and the economic incidence of the corporate income tax.

CHAPTER 16

Taxes on Consumption and Sales

Chapter Objectives: After reading and working through this chapter, you should understand:

1. The notion of, and issues related, to an expenditure tax and its justification.

2. The definition of a comprehensive consumption tax base.

3. The economic effects of a general tax on comprehensive consumption.

4. The forms and usage of sales taxes.

5. The economic effects of sales taxes.

6. The notion of a turnover tax.

7. The notion of a value-added tax.

8. The implementation and administration of value-added taxes.

Chapter Summary:

1. This chapter focuses on the feasibility of a general tax on comprehensive consumption. The advantages and disadvantages of such a tax, compared with a comprehensive income tax, are analyzed. In addition, the notion of a value-added tax, its implementation in Europe, and the feasibility of its adoption in the United States are discussed.

2. Many argue that consumption is a better index of ability to pay than is income. A direct consumption tax would involve annual declaration of consumption expenditures and calculation of the tax in a fashion similar to the personal income tax. Taxable consumption could be calculated directly from data on income, by excluding that portion of income that is saved rather than spent. This also avoids the problem of calculating changes in net worth, as must be done with a comprehensive income tax.

3. A *comprehensive consumption tax,* also called an expenditure tax, would exclude from income all savings, without limit and for any purpose. When funds are withdrawn and spent, they will be taxed. Only current expenditures are taxed under the consumption tax. Such a tax allows persons to defer the tax on their savings and eliminates any distortions from inflation.

4. Income taxes discriminate against those who defer consumption. They tend to discriminate according to the way income is timed over a person's lifetime. A tax on consumption avoids discrimination against savers by exempting their savings and interest income from taxation until they are consumed. People with equal capacity to consume are treated equally under a comprehensive consumption tax. Both the saver and the nonsaver are taxed only according to their labor income.

5. A *cash-flow tax* would allow taxpayers, in computing tax liability, to deduct from adjusted gross income all savings deposited in qualified accounts. In effect, it would broaden IRA-type deductions for a wider variety of qualified accounts (not including checking accounts). In addition, the cash-flow tax would not tax interest earned on checking and other nonqualified accounts. Loans would be added to adjusted gross income as they are received, but would be deducted from income as they are repaid.

6. The advantages and disadvantages of a general tax on comprehensive consumption may be highlighted by comparing the tax with a general tax on comprehensive income. The consumption tax would be expected to reduce or eliminate any efficiency loss in the allocation of resources between current and future consumption. The interest rate is not affected by a consumption tax. However, there will be a possibility of additional efficiency losses in labor markets. A consumption tax, due to its smaller tax base, will require a higher tax rate than an equal-yield income tax. This higher tax rate further decreases the return to work effort and increases the distortion of the work-leisure choice. Recall that the increased tax burden is more than proportionate to the increase in the tax rate. The efficiency loss in the labor market is of particular interest due to the large proportion of total income that labor income represents. Thus, the efficiency gains and losses must be carefully weighed.

7. A consumption tax is likely to be borne according to labor income. With a relatively inelastic supply of labor, the portion of the tax which could be shifted would be relatively small.

8. Sales taxes are widely used by state governments in the United States. Most of these sales taxes exempt certain items from the tax base and, in some cases, tax the purchase of capital goods. They therefore do not conform to a comprehensive consumption tax base.

9. A *retail sales tax* usually is an ad valorem levy of a fixed percentage on the dollar value of retail purchases by consumers. The retail sales tax is collected from retailers, but its burden is generally borne by consumers. Less of the tax is shifted when retail sales can migrate to neighboring jurisdictions.

10. Excise taxes are selective taxes levied on certain types of consumption activities. They are distortionary taxes. Some are designed to raise revenue, while others are intended to discourage particular consumption activities. Tariffs are an example of excise taxes.

11. Recall from Chapter 11 that minimizing the excess burden of a system of sales and excise taxes requires taxing various goods at differing rates. *Ceteris paribus*, goods should be taxed at rates that decrease with the elasticity of demand. Given the inelasticity of demand for basic necessities, such a system is not likely to be politically popular.

12. *Turnover taxes* are multistage sales taxes that are levied, at some fixed rate, on transactions at all levels of production. The effective tax rate is thus conditioned by the number of stages of production. The tax provides an incentive for vertical integration of firms. The tax usually is reflected in higher final consumption prices.

13. The *value-added tax* (VAT) is a multistage sales tax that exempts the purchase of intermediate goods and services from the tax base. It is a major source of revenue for the members of the European Union and has been seriously considered for use in the United States. Different types of value-added taxes are classified by their treatment of capital goods purchases. A product-type tax allows no deduction for initial outlays on capital goods or for amortization of the goods. An income-type tax permits a deduction for annual depreciation over the life of the equipment. A consumption-type tax allows the full cost of capital to be deducted in the year of purchase. The consumption-type tax is most common. The most common method of administering the tax is the invoice method. All transactions are taxed at a fixed proportional rate, and taxpayers are allowed to deduct the taxes paid on intermediate purchases in determining their tax liability. This requires that invoice records be maintained, hence the term invoice method.

Issue in Brief: Taxation of Services

A number of states are expanding their sales tax base to include services and service industries. As of 1998 only a few states taxed a wide array of services, but nearly all states had begun to tax some kind of service. This reflects any effort to adjust the revenue structure to reflect the now dominant, and still growing, service sector. According to U.S. Department of Commerce figures, in 1997 services accounted for 60 percent of personal consumption expenditures. Given this trend and the fiscal stress faced by government, even the staunchest opponents of sales-tax expansions expect to lose their battle.

Questions for Discussion:

1. New Mexico, Hawaii, and South Dakota successfully implemented broad-based sales taxes on services decades ago. Why was this transition relatively easier for these states than for most states today?

2. What would be some of the concerns raised about service tax expansion?

CHAPTER REVIEW QUESTIONS

True/False Questions: If false, explain how to correct the statement to make it true.

1. A general tax on consumption is equivalent to an income tax that allows savings to be excluded from the tax base.

2. Kaldor argued that income is a better index of ability to pay than is consumption.

3. Under a flat-rate tax on comprehensive income, savers would pay higher taxes over their lifetimes than individuals who consume the bulk of their income when they earn it.

4. Only current expenditures are taxed under the consumption tax.

5. Inflation is still a problem under the consumption tax.

6. Loans under the consumption tax would be taxed when received.

7. Under a cash-flow tax, deposits in checking accounts would be deductible from income.

8. In general, the tax rate under a consumption tax would have to be higher than the tax rate under an equal-yield income tax.

9. Under a consumption tax, savers incur no extra tax liability as compared with that of nonsavers.

10. A flat-rate consumption tax creates a wedge between the gross interest rate and the net interest rate.

11. A consumption tax generally will be borne according to labor earnings.

12. The consumption tax is likely to be more regressive than an equal-yield income tax.

13. Capital goods are generally exempt from sales taxes.

____ 14. The retail sales tax can be considered a general tax.

____ 15. The retail sales tax in the United States is a state and local fiscal instrument rather than a national one.

____ 16. Excise taxes are distortionary taxes.

____ 17. Tariffs that are successful revenue instruments cannot fulfill their function as protective devices for domestic industries.

____ 18. Minimizing the excess burden of a system of sales and excise taxes requires taxing all goods at the same rate.

____ 19. A turnover tax discourages vertical integration among firms.

____ 20. The most popular form of value-added tax is a product-type tax.

____ 21. As implemented in most countries, the VAT distorts the basic work-leisure choice.

____ 22. In most nations that use the VAT, it is customary not to itemize the tax on the final transaction.

____ 23. A VAT is typically rebated on export sales.

____ 24. A VAT has relatively low administrative and compliance costs.

Multiple Choice Questions: Choose the best answer.

____ 1. The federal government in the United States taxes consumption mainly through the use of:
a) income taxes.
b) retail sales taxes.
c) excise taxes.
d) turnover taxes.

____ 2. Which of the following is a criticism of an income tax?
a) Kaldor's argument that consumption is a better index of ability to pay than income.
b) It tends to discriminate according to the way income is timed over a person's lifetime.
c) Income taxation results in double taxation of savings.
d) all of the above.

____ 3. Under a consumption tax:
   a) the present value of taxes paid by savers will exceed that of the taxes paid by nonsavers.
   b) the present value of taxes paid by nonsavers will exceed that of the taxes paid by savers.
   c) savers will pay less taxes than nonsavers.
   d) nonsavers will pay less taxes than savers.

____ 4. For nonsavers, a tax on consumption:
   a) is equivalent to a tax on income.
   b) results in windfall income gains.
   c) would be preferred to a tax on wealth.
   d) none of the above.

____ 5. The comprehensive consumption tax base:
   a) includes any increases in net worth in the tax base.
   b) only includes current expenditures.
   c) requires measurement of realized capital gains.
   d) requires that inflation be accounted for in calculating the tax.
   e) all of the above.

____ 6. Loans:
   a) receive the same treatment under a general consumption tax and an income tax.
   b) are added to a taxpayer's income under an income tax.
   c) are counted as consumption when received under a general consumption tax.
   d) are taxed when they are spent under a general consumption tax.

____ 7. Under a cash-flow tax:
   a) deposits in "qualified accounts" would be subtracted from the tax base.
   b) interest earned on checking and other nonqualified accounts would not be taxed.
   c) loans would be added to adjusted gross income as they are received.
   d) purchases of durable assets by consumers would be subject to tax.
   e) all of the above.

____ 8. As compared with an equal-yield income tax, the tax rate under a consumption tax would be:
   a) about one-half as high.
   b) about the same.
   c) higher.
   d) slightly lower.

____ 9. The substitution of a flat-rate consumption tax for an equal-yield income tax:
   a) introduces a wedge between the gross interest rate and the net interest rate.
   b) has no effect on excess burden in the capital market.
   c) would restore efficiency in the market for loanable funds.
   d) would increase excess burden in the capital market.

____ 10. The substitution of a flat-rate consumption tax for an equal-yield income tax:
   a) would increase the return to work effort.
   b) would increase efficiency in the labor market.
) would further distort the work-leisure choice.
   d) none of the above.

____ 11. The consumption tax is borne according to:
   a) purchases of capital goods.
   b) labor earnings.
   c) capital earnings.
   d) accumulated wealth.

____ 12. Which of the following is not commonly exempted from the tax base of a retail sales tax?
   a) personal services.
   b) professional services.
   c) durable goods.
   d) food.

____ 13. A true retail sales tax:
   a) is an ad valorem tax.
   b) is collected from business establishments that make retail sales.
   c) is levied only on consumption at its final stage.
   d) all of the above.

____ 14. A local tax levied on items purchased in neighboring jurisdictions but used in the taxing jurisdiction is called a(n):
   a) retail sales tax.
   b) excise tax.
   c) use tax.
   d) value-added tax.

____ 15. If a retail sales tax causes sales to migrate to neighboring jurisdictions:
   a) employment and/or business profits may decrease in the taxing jurisdiction.
   b) retail prices would rise by the full amount of the tax.
   c) the tax would be fully shifted to resource owners.
   d) tax revenues may increase.
   e) none of the above.

___ 16. Minimizing the excess burden associated with a system of sales and excise taxes requires:
  a) taxing the various goods at uniform rates.
  b) taxing capital goods at higher rates than consumer goods.
  c) taxing consumer goods at higher rates than capital goods.
  d) taxing goods at rates that increase with the elasticity of demand.
  e) taxing goods at rates that decrease with the elasticity of demand.

___ 17. A common criticism of retail sales and excise taxes is that:
  a) they are progressive with respect to income.
  b) they are general taxes with no allowed exemptions.
  c) they are regressive with respect to income.
  d) they tend to be shifted backward.

___ 18. Multistage sales taxes levied at some fixed rate on transactions at all levels of production are called:
  a) excise taxes.
  b) turnover taxes.
  c) value-added taxes.
  d) consumption taxes.

___ 19. A value-added tax which allows no deduction for the cost of capital equipment in the year of purchase but permits a deduction for annual depreciation over the life of the equipment is:
  a) a product-type VAT.
  b) a consumption-type VAT.
  c) an income-type VAT.
  d) a turnover tax.

___ 20. Which of the following is generally taxed under a VAT?
  a) used equipment.
  b) royalties.
  c) food.
  d) personal services.
  e) all of the above.

Short Answer Questions: Answer in the space provided.

1. Make a list of excise taxes levied by your state and by the federal government. What is the purpose of each of these taxes?

2. Should the United States institute a value-added tax?

Problems: Be sure to show your work.

1. Do Problem 4 in your textbook. Assuming the use of 10-year straight-line depreciation, how would your answer change if a) a 15 percent product-type value-added tax, or b) a 15 percent income-type value-added tax were levied instead?

2. A government wishes to minimize the excess burden of a tax system comprised of excise taxes on hot dogs and revolvers. If the price elasticity of demand for hot dogs is .30 (in absolute value) and the price elasticity of demand for revolvers is 1.35 (in absolute value), suggest a set of tax rates for the goods which will minimize total excess burden. (Hint: You may wish to review the material related to this topic in Chapter 11.)

SKETCH ANSWERS TO CHAPTER 16

Issue in Brief:

1. Generally because these states had and have economies that are more self-contained than those in most other states.

2. Worries about "pyramiding" (i.e., paying a sales tax several times over by the time a final service is provided), having a competitive business climate if neighboring states do not tax services, the incentive for larger firms to self-produce services they previously contracted for (thereby avoiding the tax), and the taxation of interstate service transactions.

True/False:

1. T
2. F   He argued that consumption was a better index of ability to pay.
3. T
4. T
5. F   Inflation is not a problem because only current expenditures are taxed.
6. F   Loans would be taxed when the proceeds are spent.
7. F   Checking accounts would not be considered qualified accounts.
8. T
9. F   Savers do incur an extra tax liability.
10. F   There is no wedge between the interest rates with a consumption tax.
11. T
12. T
13. F   Most sales taxes include capital goods in their base.
14. F   It is not a general tax.
15. T
16. T
17. T
18. F   Goods should be taxed at differing rates.
19. F   Vertical integration is encouraged.
20. F   Consumption-type tax is most popular.
21. T
22. T
23. T
24. F   Compliance and administrative costs are high.

Multiple Choice:

1. c	6. d	11. b	16. e
2. d	7. e	12. c	17. c
3. d	8. c	13. d	18. b
4. a	9. c	14. c	19. c
5. b	10. c	15. a	20. e

Short Answer:

1. Compare your answers with those of your classmates. Excise taxes include federal taxes on gasoline, telephone service, tires, alcoholic beverages, and cigarettes. Excise taxes are generally levied for either revenue purposes or to discourage consumption of the taxed good.

2. Compare your answer with those of your classmates. Issues to consider include elimination of other taxes, implementation and administration issues, the experiences of other countries, and excess burden.

Problems:

1.
   a) No deduction would be allowed for the equipment, so the manufacturer's tax liability would now be $45,000.

   b) One year of depreciation could be claimed at a rate of $5,000, so the tax liability would now be $44,250.

2. Ramsey's rule says to equate the product of the tax rate and the price elasticity of demand across goods. Therefore, t(h)*(.30) = t(r)*(1.35). This means that t(h)/t(r) = 4.5.So, a possible burden-minimizing structure would be a 45 percent excise tax on hot dogs and a 10 percent excise tax on revolvers.

Chapter Recap: You should now be able to answer the following questions:

1. What is an expenditure tax? What is the justification for its use? How does it perform with respect to the equity criterion?

2. Define the tax base for a comprehensive consumption tax.

3. Describe the economic effects of a general tax on comprehensive consumption.

4. Discuss the various forms and uses of sales taxes.

5. What are the economic effects of sales taxes?

6. What is a turnover tax?

7. What is a value-added tax? What different forms can it take?

8. Describe the issues faced in the administration and implementation of a value-added tax.

CHAPTER 17

Taxes on Wealth, Property, and Estates

Chapter Objectives: After reading and working through this chapter, you should understand:

1. The definition of a comprehensive wealth tax base.

2. The economic effects of a comprehensive wealth tax.

3. The notion of selective property taxes and the effects of property tax differentials.

4. The notion and implications of tax capitalization.

5. The notion and justification of land taxes.

6. The various types of property transfer taxes and their economic effects.

Chapter Summary:

1. This chapter focuses on the taxation of accumulated wealth and its transfer. The wealth tax has a long history of utilization and appears to follow a cyclical course which is correlated with the economic development of a society. In its final stages, the wealth tax degenerates to a tax on real estate. The bulk of the revenue currently raised by property taxes in the United States comes from taxes on real estate. The property tax is mainly used by local governments in the United States.

2. The failure to tax wealth may allow households to escape paying taxes on consumer durables that yield nonmonetary returns which are difficult to impute and tax under an income tax. Wealth represents the value of accumulated savings and investments in a nation. Administering a wealth tax is complicated by the fact that wealth is a stock. The values of assets can change quickly and are difficult to determine for assets which are infrequently traded in markets. In addition, human wealth is nearly impossible to value.

3. A general wealth tax would tax all forms of wealth. The administrative problems encountered in taxing many forms of wealth have made selective wealth taxes much more common, hence the tendency in the United States to levy a tax on real estate while exempting other forms of wealth. *Assessment* is the valuation of taxable wealth by government authorities. Its objectivity varies from asset to asset.

4. A *comprehensive wealth tax* is one that would be levied on all forms of capital and land at a flat rate. In effect, it is levied on the discounted present value of land and capital services over time. The tax reduces interest income from all forms of accumulated savings. Its economic effects depend on the elasticity of supply of all forms of saving for the purpose of accumulating assets. With perfect inelasticity of supply of saving, the annual return to saving would drop by the full amount of the tax. The tax would be borne in accordance with the ownership of wealth. When the supply of saving is not perfectly inelastic, some of the burden of the tax will be shifted to nonsavers in the form of higher interest rates and their general equilibrium effects. Excess burden will also be higher when the supply of savings is responsive.

5. Compared with equal-yield consumption or income taxes, a general wealth tax is more detrimental to the saving incentive, but less detrimental to the work incentive.

6. Taxes on real assets account for about 80 percent of all revenue collected from property tax levies in the United States. Taxes on real estate provide incentives to substitute alternative inputs for real property. In addition, locational adjustments are induced by differentials between the property tax rates in competing jurisdictions. A national tax on real property would be borne by owners of all forms of capital, in much the same way as the corporation income tax in the Harberger model.

7. The tax rate differentials above or below the average rate of taxation among jurisdictions can be avoided by reallocation of investment from high- to low-tax jurisdictions. Some shifting of the tax to noncapital input owners takes place in the process. In areas where investment declines, lower land rents and lower wages are a logical outcome. This shifting is most likely to occur in regions of above-average income.

8. *Tax capitalization* is a decrease in the value of a taxed asset that reflects the discounted present value of future tax liability for its owners. The extent of capitalization depends on the degree to which owners of the taxed asset can adjust the amounts available in response to the tax. The magnitude of any price reduction varies directly with the anticipated life span of the asset, and inversely with the elasticity of supply of the asset. Empirical research has indicated marked capitalization of both intergovernmental and interjurisdictional property tax differentials.

9. Considerable controversy exists concerning the incidence of the property tax in the United States. One view says that the property tax is basically an excise tax on housing, and is thus a regressive tax. An alternative view argues that the tax is borne in the form of a lower return to all uses of capital, and thus the tax is progressive in its impact. The burden of regional redistribution of investment in response to property tax differentials is argued to further contribute to the tax's progressivity.

10. Support is often voiced for substituting a land tax in the place of the tax on real estate. Such a tax would be equivalent to a lump-sum tax and would remove disincentives to land development and redevelopment. Unfortunately, such a tax would yield only small amounts of revenue, even at very high tax rates.

11. *Property transfer taxes* are levied on transfers of wealth among citizens. They include estate, inheritance, and gift taxes. Each of these taxes generally includes large exemptions and deductions. As taxes on accumulated savings as those savings are transferred, the taxes probably have some effect in reducing the willingness of individuals to transfer accumulated wealth to others. Nevertheless, the tax on the transfer is generally lower than would be the case if it were treated as capital income to the recipient. Recent evidence suggests that the estate tax may actually increase income inequality if saving is responsive to the tax rates for the estate tax.

Issue in Brief: Senior Citizen Tax Break

Many states give special property tax preferences to the elderly. For example, in late 1994, the Illinois General Assembly froze property assessments of lower income elderly homeowners. The legislation froze property tax assessments at 1994 levels for homeowners 65 and older who have annual incomes of $35,000 or less. More than a half million elderly homeowners were expected to be eligible at the program's inception. The Illinois Department of Revenue estimated that taxing districts in the state (n.b., Illinois has far more units of local government than any other state) would lose $26.6 million in revenue next year as a result of the legislation. The annual loss would soar to an estimated $251.1 million by 2002. These revenue losses are that much more severe in the presence of the property tax extension limitations that apply to the most populous area of the state as a result of 1991 and 1995 legislation.

Questions for Discussion:

1. Who are some of the losers under this legislation?

2. Can senior citizens' tax bills still go up under this law? How?

3. Why might one argue that an assessment freeze for the elderly is generally unnecessary?

CHAPTER REVIEW QUESTIONS

True/False Questions: If false, explain how to correct the statement to make it true.

____ 1. The property tax is mainly used by state governments in the United States.

____ 2. Wealth is a stock, while income and consumption are flows.

____ 3. Failure to subtract all debt incurred by households in calculating the wealth tax base results in double counting of assets.

____ 4. Taxes on real estate are relatively easy to evade.

____ 5. A general wealth tax can be thought of as being levied on the discounted present value of land and capital services over time.

____ 6. A general wealth tax reduces the annual return to all forms of saving.

____ 7. When the supply of savings is responsive, a wealth tax would result in a decline in the gross return to savings and investment.

____ 8. A general wealth tax has an adverse effect on the return to work effort.

____ 9. A selective wealth tax is a distortionary tax.

____ 10. Other things being equal, those local governments where property tax rates are lower than the national average can expect a reduction in local investment.

____ 11. Property tax differentials can be shifted to noncapital input owners.

____ 12. Property tax differentials are often capitalized into property values.

____ 13. The magnitude of reduction in asset price due to tax capitalization decreases as the anticipated life span of the asset increases.

____ 14. Empirical research concludes that there is little capitalization of tax differentials among communities.

____ 15. The incidence of property taxes on commercial property is borne by landlords and investors.

____ 16. Under fractional assessment, the property tax rate understates the real rate of taxation.

____ 17. If the property tax is viewed as a sales tax on housing, the tax would appear to be regressive with respect to income.

____ 18. Regional reallocation of capital causes land rents in low-tax jurisdictions to increase.

____ 19. A land tax would have positive excess burden.

____ 20. Many states offer preferential tax treatment for land used in agriculture.

____ 21. Bequests to charitable foundations are taxable under estate and inheritance taxes.

____ 22. Estates may be left to the surviving spouse, exempt of all property transfer taxes.

____ 23. Property transfer tax effective tax rates are low relative to the statutory rates.

____ 24. Recent analysis suggests that the estate tax may increase income inequality.

Multiple Choice Questions: Choose the best answer.

____ 1. Which of the following appears earliest in the property-tax cycle?
   a) a per-unit levy on land alone.
   b) a proportional tax on the holding of all wealth.
   c) a real property tax.
   d) a selective tax on personal property.

____ 2. Which of the following complicates the administration of a wealth tax?
   a) the value of the taxable assets must be determined at a particular point in time.
   b) it is difficult to determine the value of assets that are infrequently traded on markets.
   c) the value of assets can change quite rapidly.
   d) all of the above.

____ 3. Total wealth includes:
   a) real property.
   b) tangible personal property.
   c) intangible personal property.
   d) human capital.
   e) all of the above.

____ 4. A tax on which of the following would be hardest to evade?
   a) securities.
   b) real estate.
   c) jewelry.
   d) art work.

____ 5. Valuation of taxable wealth by government authorities is called:
   a) comparable worth.
   b) attachment of assets.
   c) assessment.
   d) capitalization.
   e) none of the above.

____ 6. Which of the following statements is false?
   a) A general wealth tax can be thought of as being levied on the discounted present value of land and capital services over time.
   b) A general wealth tax reduces interest income from accumulated savings.
   c) It is reasonable to assume that the demand for capital is perfectly inelastic.
   d) A general wealth tax creates no distortion in allocation between different types of savings.

____ 7. A proportional general tax on wealth when the supply of savings is perfectly inelastic:
   a) will reduce the return to savings by a portion of the amount of the tax.
   b) will distort the choice between types of saving.
   c) will reduce the return to savings by the full amount of the tax.
   d) will have no excess burden.

____ 8. A proportional general tax on wealth when the supply of savings is responsive:
   a) would increase the gross return to saving and investment.
   b) would result in greater losses in efficiency in investment markets than in the case when the supply of savings is perfectly inelastic.
   c) would be shifted to people other than savers.
   d) all of the above.

____ 9. As compared with an equal-yield consumption or income tax, a general wealth tax:
   a) results in more distortion in investment markets, but has no effect on the return to work effort.
   b) results in more distortion in both investment and labor markets.
   c) results in less distortion in investment markets, but greater distortion in labor markets.
   d) results in less distortion in both investment and labor markets.

____ 10. A national tax on real property would be borne by:
   a) owners of noncapital resources.
   b) owners of all forms of capital.
   c) owners of real property.
   d) none of the above.

____ 11. Which of the following statements about property tax differentials is false?
   a) Tax rate differentials result in reallocation of investment.
   b) These differentials can be shifted to noncapital input owners.
   c) Land rents would rise in low-tax jurisdictions as investment is reallocated.
   d) The prices of locally produced services in high-tax jurisdictions would drop as investment is reallocated.
   e) Housing costs would fall in low-tax areas as investment is reallocated.

____ 12. A decrease in the value of a taxed asset that reflects the discounted present value of future tax liability of its owners is:
   a) tax evasion.
   b) tax capitalization.
   c) tax avoidance.
   d) tax indexation.

____ 13. Which of the following affects the degree of tax capitalization?
   a) the elasticity of supply of the taxed asset.
   b) the anticipated life span of the asset.
   c) the economy's discount rate.
   d) all of the above.

____ 14. Under fractional assessment, the statutory property tax rate:
   a) overstates the real rate of taxation.
   b) understates the real rate of taxation.
   c) is equal to the effective tax rate.
   d) none of the above.

____ 15. Empirical evidence indicates that assessment ratios:
   a) often exceed 100 percent.
   b) decline with increases in home values.
   c) increase with increases in home values.
   d) are relatively uniform nationally.

___ 16. Economic theory suggests:
   a) the property tax is equivalent to a tax on the consumption of housing.
   b) the burden of the local property tax is likely to be regressive with respect to income.
   c) the burden of the local property tax is likely to be proportional with respect to income.
   d) the burden of the local property tax is likely to be progressive with respect to income.

___ 17. The use of state income tax credits to offset some of the burden of local property taxes is called:
   a) tax capitalization.
   b) tax unification.
   c) a circuit-breaker.
   d) an exemption.

___ 18. A land tax:
   a) is a distortionary tax.
   b) has no effect on land prices.
   c) would have progressive redistributive effects.
   d) is equivalent to a lump-sum tax.

___ 19. Which of the following statements about land taxes is false?
   a) Agricultural land is often given preferential treatment.
   b) The tax generally yields large amounts of revenue.
   c) It would be expected to result in a more efficient land use pattern.
   d) It would provide incentives for land development.

___ 20. Which of the following is not a property transfer tax?
   a) gift tax.
   b) inheritance tax.
   c) personal property tax.
   d) estate tax.

Short Answer Questions: Answer in the space provided.

1. Make a list of your total wealth. Be sure to include any accumulated human capital. What type of wealth does each of your assets represent?

2. Using the list your made in Question 1, assess the value of your wealth. Note the method by which you valued each of your assets. Which assets would be difficult to tax? Why?

Problems: Be sure to show your work.

1. You are given the following information about a closed local economy: Real property owned by households is valued at $5 million; tangible personal property owned by households is valued at $2 million; intangible personal property owned by households consists of $1 million in local government bonds, $2 million in corporate bonds, and $1 million in corporate stock; corporate assets are valued at $3 million; and debt incurred by households totals $1 million. If the statutory local property tax rate is a uniform 2 percent levied on all forms of net wealth, how much revenue will the local government raise from the tax?

2. Do Problem 4 in your textbook. How would your answer change if the land had a finite, three-year life? Does this agree with the theory suggested in your textbook regarding the relationship between the drop in market value and asset life?

SKETCH ANSWERS TO CHAPTER 17

Issue in Brief:

1. Young homeowners, elderly renters, and taxing districts are all losers.

2. Yes, because the assessment level is frozen, but a higher tax rate applied to the frozen assessment would still result in a higher tax bill.

3. Rising assessments are generally a function of increasing property values and property taxes generally only capture a small portion of the increase in this value. Therefore, on balance an increase in assessment should not be indicative of decreased ability to pay if wealth is considered.

True/False:

1. F   It is used primarily by local governments.
2. T
3. T
4. F   These taxes are difficult to evade.
5. T
6. T
7. F   The gross return would increase.

8. F The return to work effort is unaffected.
9. T
10. F They can expect an increase in investment.
11. T
12. T
13. F The reduction in price varies directly with the anticipated life span of the asset.
14. F Research concludes that capitalization is significant.
15. T
16. F The real rate is overstated.
17. T
18. T
19. F A land tax would have no excess burden.
20. T
21. F They are exempt from tax.
22. T
23. T
24. T

Multiple Choice:

1.	a	6.	c	11.	d	16.	d
2.	d	7.	c	12.	b	17.	c
3.	e	8.	d	13.	d	18.	d
4.	b	9.	a	14.	a	19.	b
5.	c	10.	b	15.	b	20.	c

Short Answer:

1. Compare your answers with those of your classmates. Recall that wealth can be divided into real property, tangible personal property, intangible personal property, and human capital.

2. Compare your answers with those of your classmates. Be sure to discuss the degree of subjectivity in your assessments. Recall that moveable, nonregistered assets can be easy to hide, and that taxation requires the ability to assess the value of assets in a defensible fashion.

Problems:

1. The taxable base is $10 million. Thus, the revenue raised would be $200,000. The tax base would either exclude intangible household property representing claims on the assets of corporations *or* exclude corporate assets. Debt incurred by households would also reduce the tax base.

2. The post-tax value with an infinite life is $66,666.66. The pre-tax value with three-year life is $24,868.52, and the post-tax value is $22,832.24. Thus, the drop in value is smaller for the asset with a finite life, consistent with theory.

Chapter Recap: You should now be able to answer the following questions:

1. How is the tax base of a comprehensive wealth tax defined?

2. Discuss the economic effects of a comprehensive wealth tax.

3. What is a selective property tax? What are some examples of selective
    property taxes?

4. What are property tax differentials? Why are they important?

5. What is tax capitalization? What are its implications?

6. What is a land tax? How is a land tax typically justified? What are its disadvantages?

7. Discuss the various types of property transfer taxes utilized in the United States. What is the nature of their economic effects?

CHAPTER 18

Fiscal Federalism and State and Local Government Finance

Chapter Objectives: After reading and working through this chapter, you should understand:

1. The notion of fiscal federalism.

2. The notion of a local public good.

3. The notion and consequences of interjurisdictional externalities.

4. The basic assumptions and implications of the Tiebout model.

5. The elasticity of the local tax base and the constraints it imposes on state and local government tax policy.

6. The nature and implications of tax competition and tax exporting.

7. The notion of fiscal capacity and its variation among state and local governments.

8. The notion of revenue effort.

9. The notion of intergovernmental grants and the forms such grants take.

10. The economic justification and economic effects of intergovernmental grants.

11. The issues regarding state and local government finance of education in the United States.

Chapter Summary:

1. *Fiscal federalism* is the division of taxing and expenditure functions among levels of government. This chapter focuses on issues related to state and local government finance in a federal system, the allocation of responsibilities among alternative levels of government, and current issues and challenges inherent in state and local government finance.

2. The proportion of the population for which the benefits of a public good are nonrival helps to determine the appropriate level of government that should provide the good. Those functions which have benefits which are collectively consumed at the national level, or require central coordination in provision, will likely be undertaken by the central government. *Local public goods* are public goods whose benefits are nonrival only for a portion of the national population living within a certain geographical area. Such goods will be supplied by subnational governments, with the appropriate level determined by the scale and diversity of the benefits.

3. Local and regional supply and finance of government-provided services allows the system of governments to accommodate a wide array of tastes and demands for their services. It offers citizens the opportunity to consider a menu of services offered at alternative locations in choosing a residence. In addition, decentralized collective choices can improve the efficiency of government output, especially with respect to local public goods.

4. The basic problem of fiscal federalism is to determine the efficient political jurisdictions for the responsibility of deciding how much of and what kinds of government-provided goods and services to produce. One factor that influences the assignment of functions to levels of government is the desire to avoid or minimize *interjurisdictional externalities*, that is, costs or benefits of local government goods and services which flow to residents of other political jurisdictions. Ideally, jurisdictional boundaries could be set up such that each good was provided at a level appropriate to the elimination of any spillovers. However, there are significant transaction costs in setting up the numerous governing authorities which would be necessary.

5. The Tiebout model argues, under a set of restricting assumptions, that a quasi-market equilibrium in residential location is achieved as citizens move to communities whose government budget best satisfies their own preferences for public services, subject to the constraint that all communities are providing public services at minimum unit costs. The Tiebout model is relevant because, at least at the margin, some households do respond to differences among government budgets in alternative communities. Nevertheless, the actual equilibrium residential choice pattern is not an efficient one due to interjurisdictional externalities and the failure of the real world to reflect Tiebout's assumptions.

6. Local taxing authorities are very concerned about the elasticity of the local tax base. Among the factors that affect the elasticity of the tax base are the degree of mobility of taxed resources, the rates of taxation applied to similar tax bases in surrounding communities, and the relative amount of revenues collected. In addition, the services financed influence locational choices by economic agents. The mobility of economic agents also means that taxes may vary in terms of their efficiency effects depending on the level at which they are imposed. The tax base is also likely to become more elastic over time.

7. The elasticity of the tax base is the ratio of the percentage change in the tax base attributable to any given percentage change in the tax rate applied to that base. Tax-base elasticity is determined by the ability to engage in substitute nontaxed activities, the ability to move to a jurisdiction without the tax, and the ability and willingness to engage in other forms of tax avoidance or evasion.

8. The elasticity of tax bases often results in competition among governmental units for residents and business firms whose economic activities increase the units' tax bases. Such competition often constrains the size of local public budgets. One way of reducing the burden of local taxation is through tax exporting. Tax exporting refers to the shifting of the burden of local taxes to nonresidents. Tax exporting is very common in many resort communities.

9. *Fiscal capacity* is a measure of the ability of a jurisdiction to finance government-provided services. The fiscal capacities of local jurisdictions are likely to vary with the values of local tax bases, as well as with the ability to export taxes and the elasticity of the tax base. Fiscal capacity measures are often used as an input in formulas determining the magnitudes of intergovernmental grants designed to redistribute purchasing power among political jurisdictions.

10. *Revenue effort* is the ratio of tax collections from all sources in a taxing jurisdiction, as a percentage of personal income in that jurisdiction, to the national average of that ratio for all jurisdictions. Unfortunately, revenue effort is a very crude measure with numerous determinants. It also ignores the revenue side of the budget.

11. Intergovernmental aid is an important source of revenue for many state and local governments. Not only does it help to ensure minimum levels of certain public services in all regions of a country, but it also helps to internalize interjurisdictional externalities and to meet a variety of social objectives.

12. The major types of grants are categorical grants, block grants, and general purpose grants. Categorical grants have specified conditions attached to the expenditure of the funds. Most have matching requirements which require governments to share the costs of the program. Block grants restrict expenditures, but only within the broad constraints of general program areas. General purpose grants, also called unconditional grants, have no strings attached. In recent years, there has been an increased tendency to try to use block grants in the place of both its more restrictive and less restrictive cousins. The fungibility of money somewhat reduces the distinction between the types of grants.

13. Intergovernmental aid represents subsidies from one level of government to another level. These subsidies can be expected to affect the political equilibrium in a fashion analogous to the effects of subsidies on consumer equilibrium. Matching grants have both income and substitution effects and are more likely to stimulate expanded production of public goods than nonmatching grants, grants that only result in income effects.

Issue in Brief: School Finance Reform

One of the hottest issues of fiscal federalism in recent years has been the financing of primary and secondary education. Due to court challenges, the tax and expenditure limitation movement, civil rights concerns, and other varying factors, an increasing number of states have transferred significant funding authority for schools to the state level. One of the most drastic recent reforms was in Michigan where the state implemented a statewide property tax system that generally replaces the local property tax finance of education in most school districts (and greatly reduces the property tax burden for most homeowners), raised the state sales tax from 4% to 6%, raised the cigarette tax from $.25 to $.75 per pack, implements a new 6% tax on out-of-state phone calls, and reduces the state personal income tax rate from 4.6% to 4.4%. This tax reform will help better balance the revenue system in the state, making Michigan more competitive with its neighboring states, and reduce interlocal tax differentials that the state believed were detrimentally affecting the distribution of economic activity within the state. On the education side of the equation, the reforms are expected to help reduce the inequities between school districts that were the result of a school finance system dependent on locally generated revenues. The state will now finance a basic level of education in all districts from statewide revenues. For further information, see Paul D. Ballew, Richard H. Mattoon, and William A. Testa, *Chicago Fed Letter*, Federal Reserve Bank of Chicago, May 1994.

Questions for Discussion:

1. Has your state implemented any school finance reform legislation in recent years? What does it do?

2. With statewide finance comes the possibility of increased state control. From what you have learned in this chapter, would this change be consistent with public finance theory?

3. Some people have argued that increased funds for schools should only come after significant accountability measures are introduced into the system. What might be some accountability measures that could be introduced?

CHAPTER REVIEW QUESTIONS

True/False Questions: If false, explain how to correct the statement to make it true.

_____ 1. No one state can stabilize its own inflation and unemployment rates.

_____ 2. It is easier to avoid federal taxes than state and local taxes.

_____ 3. Under decentralized collective choices made by majority rule, the political equilibrium reflects the median most-preferred outcome of national voters.

_____ 4. The tax and expenditure decisions in one governing jurisdiction are not independent of those in other jurisdictions.

_____ 5. In a federal system of government, political jurisdictions are both centralized and decentralized.

_____ 6. The transaction costs associated with having many governing authorities may limit the desirability of internalizing interjurisdictional externalities.

_____ 7. There can be positive interjurisdictional externalities when the jurisdiction comprises all citizens.

_____ 8. In the Tiebout model, an optimum community size is defined as that which corresponds to minimum unit costs of government services.

_____ 9. The Tiebout model is useful in partially explaining suburbanization in the United States.

_____ 10. The Tiebout model is useful in explaining interstate moves.

_____ 11. Local property tax policy can affect the value of the property tax base.

_____ 12. Taxes that are neutral when imposed at the national level will be neutral when imposed at the local level.

_____ 13. Taxes that account for a very small percentage of taxpayers' income are likely to have elastic tax bases with respect to the rate of taxation.

_____ 14. Taxes on nonlodging expenditures by tourists are more likely to be exported than taxes on hotel rooms.

_____ 15. Deductibility of state and local taxes under the federal personal income tax can lead to tax exportation.

____ 16. Tax competition often constrains the sizes of local public budgets.

____ 17. Fiscal capacity increases with the ability to "export" taxes.

____ 18. Jurisdictions with low levels of personal income require a lower revenue effort to maintain the same level of per-capita expenditure than do jurisdictions that have high levels of personal income.

____ 19. One limitation of revenue effort is that it does not reflect differences in collective choices among communities with respect to the allocation of resources between public and private use.

____ 20. A categorical grant-in-aid has few conditions attached to the expenditure of the funds.

____ 21. Medicaid is a categorical grant-in-aid program.

____ 22. If there are opportunities for communities to engage in bargaining to internalize externalities, then categorical grants may be unnecessary and their use could result in inefficiencies.

____ 23. The distinction between restricted and unrestricted grants is enhanced by the fungibility of money.

____ 24. Most categorical grants have matching requirements.

____ 25. Federal grants account for a larger proportion of federal expenditures now than they did in 1980.

____ 26. In general, matching grants are more expansionary than nonmatching grants in terms of increased output on the part of recipient governments.

____ 27. Categorical grants, without matching requirements, result in only income effects.

____ 28. In general, no great correlation exists between total federal grants received and per-capita income among states.

Multiple Choice Questions: Choose the best answer.

____ 1. A system of government characterized by numerous levels of government, each with its own powers to provide services and raise revenue is called:
   a) democratic.
   b) federal.
   c) socialist.
   d) republican.
   e) none of the above.

____ 2. Which of the following government-supplied goods and services is least likely to be efficiently provided by local governments?
   a) economic stabilization programs.
   b) police protection.
   c) fire protection.
   d) roads.

____ 3. Public goods whose benefits are nonrival only for a portion of the national population living within a certain geographical area are called:
   a) congestible public goods.
   b) limited public goods.
   c) local public goods.
   d) pure public goods.

____ 4. Which of the following government-supplied goods and services is likely to be efficiently produced by local government?
   a) public sanitation and refuse collection.
   b) educational services.
   c) fire protection.
   d) water and sewer services.
   e) all of the above.

____ 5. Localized collective choice:
   a) provides more flexibility and improves efficiency because government output can respond to variations in tastes.
   b) allows governments to adjust their tax structures so as to attain notions of fairness in taxation which may vary across jurisdictions.
   c) results in a political equilibrium which reflects the median most-preferred outcome of local voters.
   d) all of the above.

____ 6. Which of the following is not a political jurisdiction?
   a) Los Angeles County.
   b) Illinois.
   c) North America.
   d) West Dundee Fire Protection District.
   e) none of the above.

____ 7. Costs or benefits of local government goods and services which flow to residents who live in other political jurisdictions are called:
   a) congestion.
   b) universalities.
   c) pecuniary externalities.
   d) interjurisdictional externalities.
   e) technological externalities.

____ 8. Which of the following is not an assumption of the Tiebout model?
   a) Communities vary in the employment opportunities they offer.
   b) Citizens are fully mobile among communities.
   c) Citizens possess full knowledge of government budgets in alternative political jurisdictions.
   d) There are no interjurisdictional externalities.
   e) none of the above.

____ 9. Optimum community size in the Tiebout model:
   a) minimizes the per capita unit costs of government services.
   b) assures all citizens can live in their first-choice community.
   c) is that which corresponds to minimum unit costs of government services.
   d) is such that communities above the optimal size try to encourage new residents.
   e) all of the above.

____ 10. The Tiebout model would likely be most useful in explaining:
   a) movements of households from downtown Boston to Boston suburbs.
   b) movements of households from West Germany to the United States.
   c) movements of households from the snowbelt to the sunbelt.
   d) The model is equally applicable to each of these cases.

____ 11. For which of the following government-provided goods and services are interjurisdictional externalities likely to be significant?
   a) streets and road networks.
   b) public transit.
   c) pollution control.
   d) cultural facilities.
   e) all of the above.

____ 12. Governmental consolidation:
   a) allows internalization of interjurisdictional externalities.
   b) may reduce the costs per unit of government output.
   c) may increase the costs per unit of government activity.
   d) may be either full or partial.
   e) all of the above.

____ 13. Which of the following is not a determinant of the elasticity of the local tax base?
   a) national tax rates.
   b) the degree of mobility of taxed resources.
   c) the public services supplied by surrounding communities.
   d) the percentage of taxpayers' income the tax represents.
   e) the rates of taxation applied to similar tax bases in surrounding communities.

____   14. Over time, a local tax base is likely to:
a) account for a higher percentage of taxpayers' income.
b) account for a smaller percentage of taxpayers' income.
c) become more elastic.
d) become more inelastic.

____   15. Tax exportation arises through:
a) reduced income of out-of-state input owners who employ their inputs in the state's taxing jurisdiction.
b) increases in the price of goods and services purchased by out-of-state individuals.
c) deductibility of state and local taxes under the federal personal income tax.
d) all of the above.

____   16. Which of the following statements about tax exportation is true?
a) States with a relatively low proportion of capital input owned by out-of-state residents will tend to export state corporate income taxes and business property taxes.
b) Business taxes appear to be more easily exported than are personal taxes.
c) Analysis of a hotel room occupancy tax in Hawaii indicates that the tax is not exported to any significant extent.
d) all of the above.

____   17. Which of the following types of political jurisdictions is most likely to be a net exporter of taxes?
a) a small, self-sufficient community.
b) a resort community.
c) a nation with little foreign investment or trade.
d) a retirement community in the sunbelt.

____   18. Provision of which of the following requires a national collective decision?
a) roads.
b) education.
c) defense.
d) sanitation services.

____   19. Which of the following is a measure of the ability of a jurisdiction to finance government-provided services?
a) revenue effort.
b) tax exportation.
c) fiscal capacity.
d) the elasticity of supply for investment.

_____ 20. A value for revenue effort that is greater than 100 percent:
  a) may mean that citizens in the taxing jurisdiction have relatively strong demands for local government-supplied services compared with citizens in other jurisdictions.
  b) may mean that the community has a relatively low level of per-capita income.
  c) may mean that unique characteristics of the community require that greater per-capita expenditures be made in order to meet the basic demands for government-provided services.
  d) all of the above.

_____ 21. Which of the following types of grants has the least strings attached to the use of the funds?
  a) general revenue sharing.
  b) categorical grants-in-aid.
  c) block grants.
  d) matching grants.

_____ 22. Federal grants-in-aid accounts for about what percent of state and local government revenue?
  a) 10.
  b) 20.
  c) 40.
  d) 60.

_____ 23. The fact that funds from a grant may end up being used for any purpose even though they were intended for a specific use refers to the concept of:
  a) fraud.
  b) fungibility.
  c) embezzlement.
  d) political disequilibrium.

_____ 24. Federal grants-in-aid account for about what percent of federal outlays?
  a) 5.
  b) 15.
  c) 25.
  d) 45.

_____ 25. Matching grants:
  a) have only substitution effects.
  b) have only income effects.
  c) have both income and substitution effects.
  d) have neither income nor substitution effects.

____ 26. The bypassing of the normal political process by local bureaucrats is
called:
   a) the transfer effect.
   b) the flypaper effect.
   c) the universality principle.
   d) interjurisdictional inconclusiveness.

____ 27. The use of grants to adjust for differences in the capacity to finance
basic government-provided services among jurisdictions is called:
   a) "the Robin Hood effect."
   b) normalization.
   c) fiscal federalism.
   d) fiscal equalization.

Short Answer Questions: Answer in the space provided.

1. Make a list of taxes you pay which are levied by governmental units at a
lower level than the federal government. Discuss the elasticity of each tax
base. Does the choice of taxes seem to be linked to the perceived elasticity of
the tax base?

2. Discuss the issue of tax competition as it relates to political jurisdictions in your geographic area. Does the pattern of economic activity seem to respond to this tax competition?

3. Make a list of state and local government programs which are financed in whole or in part by intergovernmental aid. Why is intergovernmental aid used in each of these cases?

Problems: Be sure to show your work.

1. Town A has a population of 125,000 residents and Town B has a population of 150,000 residents. Town A proposes to consolidate with Town B in the provision of sewage disposal and fire protection services. You are a voter in Town B and are asked to cast votes on consolidation for each service separately (that is, assume that a special district for each service is being voted on). How would you vote?

2. Do Problem 4 in your textbook. How would your answer change if the federal government paid 85 percent of the cost?

3. How would your answers in Problem 2 change if road paving were an inferior good?

SKETCH ANSWERS TO CHAPTER 18

Issue in Brief:

1. Compare your answers with those of your classmates. Do a little library research and see what is happening in nearby states or areas.

2. Educational services are generally thought to be a local public good. To the extent that this is true, financing should probably be carried out locally. This also allows governments to provide different levels of educational services and people to "vote with their feet" to locate in the jurisdiction that best offers the service menu they desire. The Michigan system still preserves this option to some extent by only financing a basic level of education on a statewide basis, and then allowing enhancement of educational services at local option and through local funding (that must be targeted to homeowners rather than businesses in the locality).

3. Some of the most common accountability measures are based on educational outcomes, purchasing guidelines, and ratios of allowable administrative costs as a percentage of per pupil spending.

True/False:

1. T
2. F   It is easier to avoid state and local taxes.
3. F   The equilibrium reflects the median most-preferred outcome of local voters.
4. T
5. T
6. T
7. F   There can be no interjurisdictional externalities.
8. T
9. T
10. F   It is useful in explaining movements within a more constrained geographical area.
11. T
12. F   The taxes can have distorting effects when imposed on the local level.
13. F   The tax base is likely to be inelastic.
14. F   Taxes on nonlodging expenditures are less likely to be exported.
15. T
16. T
17. T
18. F   Jurisdictions with low income require a greater revenue effort to maintain a given level of per-capita expenditure.
19. F   Revenue effort does reflect such differences.
20. F   Conditions are specific and generally restrictive.
21. T
22. T
23. F   The distinction is eroded by fungibility.
24. T

25. F   Grants, as a proportion of federal expenditure, peaked in 1980.
26. T
27. T
28. T

Multiple Choice:

1. b	7. d	13. a	19. c	25. c
2. a	8. a	14. c	20. d	26. b
3. c	9. c	15. d	21. a	27. d
4. e	10. a	16. b	22. b	
5. d	11. e	17. b	23. b	
6. c	12. e	18. c	24. b	

Short Answer:

1. Compare your answers with those of your classmates. Remember to include taxes which are levied by special districts.

2. Compare your answers with those of your classmates. Look for signs of constraints in local public budgets. Have tax limitation movements had any effect on tax competition in your area?

3. Compare your answers with those of your classmates. Be sure to give consideration to the issues of the efficient jurisdiction for service provision, interjurisdictional externalities, fiscal equalization, and fiscal capacity.

Problems:

1. You are given very little information here, but empirical evidence suggests that economies of scale extend beyond 100,000 residents (and further) for sewage disposal, and evidence on fire protection suggests that diseconomies of scale can set in (some evidence suggests that this does not happen until a jurisdiction size of about 300,000 residents). Thus, an argument can be made for a yes vote for a sewage disposal district and a no vote for a fire protection district. Of course, more information about interjurisdictional externalities, the possibility of political externalities, and the costs of reduced political participation would be helpful in order to make a more informed decision.

2. The differential effect of the matching grant program would be greater. A larger increase in production of road paving would be induced. In terms of Figure 18.1, budget line AC gets shallower and shallower with increases in the federal government's share of the costs. This would increase the equilibrium quantity of road paving, assuming conventionally-shaped indifference curves.

3. The effect of the nonmatching grant would be to reduce the amount of road paving consumed. Due to the substitution effect, the matching grant would still increase consumption of road paving, assuming road paving is not a Giffen good.

Chapter Recap: You should now be able to answer the following questions:

1. What is fiscal federalism?

2. What is a local public good? What are the implications of local public goods in terms of collective choice?

3. Discuss the notion and consequences of interjurisdictional externalities.

4. What is the Tiebout model? Discuss its implications and assumptions.

5. Explain the notion of the elasticity of the local tax base. What constraints does it impose on state and local government tax policy?

6. Discuss the nature and implications of tax competition.

7. What is tax exporting? What factors affect a jurisdiction's ability to export taxes? What are the implications of tax exporting?

8. What is meant by fiscal capacity? How does fiscal capacity vary among state and local governments?

9. What is meant by revenue effort? What are the limitations of this measure?

10. What is an intergovernmental grant? What are some of the different forms that intergovernmental aid can take?

11. Discuss the economic justification for, and the economic effects of, intergovernmental grants.

12. Carefully discuss some of the major fiscal problems facing state and local governments in the United States.